REPORT NO. 28

THE NEGRO
IN THE FURNITURE INDUSTRY

by

WILLIAM E. FULMER

Published by

INDUSTRIAL RESEARCH UNIT
The Wharton School
University of Pennsylvania

Distributed by

University of Pennsylvania Press
Philadelphia, Pennsylvania 19174

Copyright © 1973 by the Trustees of the University of Pennsylvania
Library of Congress Catalog Card Number 72-94211
Manufactured in the United States of America
ISBN: 0-8122-9080-1

Foreword

In September 1966, the Ford Foundation announced a major grant to the Industrial Research Unit of the Wharton School to fund studies of the Racial Policies of American Industry. The purpose of the research effort, now in its sixth year, is to determine why some industries are more hospitable to the employment of Negroes than are others and why some companies within the same industry have vastly different racial employment policies, and to propose appropriate policy.

The studies have proceeded on an industry-by-industry basis, under the direction of the undersigned, with Dr. Richard L. Rowan, Associate Professor of Industry, as Associate Director. This study of the furniture industry is the twenty-eighth in a series of reports dealing with specific industries. Reports already published, or in press, are listed on the back cover.

In addition to individual industry reports, major studies combining and comparing the findings of the various industry reports are being completed. Volume I, *Negro Employment in Basic Industry*; Volume II, *Negro Employment in Finance*; Volume III, *Negro Employment in Public Utilities*; Volume IV, *Negro Employment in Southern Industry*; Volume V, *Negro Employment in Land and Air Transport*; and Volume VI, *Negro Employment in Retail Trade*, have all been published.

This study deals with a highly fragmented, southern-concentrated industry, the racial policies of which appear to be most affected by labor market conditions. The author, William E. Fulmer, is a doctoral candidate at the University of Pennsylvania and a Research Associate in the Industrial Research Unit. Prior to this, he received his M.B.A. from Florida State University and was employed as an industrial relations specialist by the U. S. Atomic Energy Commission.

Many persons assisted in the making of this study. Dr. John R. Coleman, President of Haverford College and a former member of the Ford Foundation staff, made the original grant possible. Subsequent grants were greatly furthered by the fine cooperation of Mitchell Sviridoff, Vice-President, and Basil J. Whiting, Program Officer, Social Development. Numerous com-

iii

pany, union, and association officials in the furniture industry generously provided time for interviews and supplied valuable information.

Miss Elsa Klemp of the Industrial Research Unit staff tabulated the statistical data and the manuscript was typed by Mrs. Louise Morrison, Mrs. Veronica M. Kent, and Miss Sharon Cox. Mrs. Margaret E. Doyle managed the various administrative details with her usual competence.

The author, of course, accepts basic responsibility for the content. As in most previous reports, the data cited as "in the author's possession" have been carefully authenticated and are on file in the Industrial Research Unit library.

HERBERT R. NORTHRUP, *Director*
Industrial Research Unit
The Wharton School
University of Pennsylvania

Philadelphia

January 1973

TABLE OF CONTENTS

LIST OF TABLES

TABLE   PAGE

CHAPTER I

Introduction

Today within the United States alone, nearly 500,000 people and more than 5,000 companies are involved in the manufacture of furniture to supply an annual retail market of $9 billion. This manufacturing activity is not of recent origins but predates our existence as a nation, thus being one of our oldest industries. If, as some have suggested, the "existence of a furniture-manufacturing industry is characteristic of an advanced and sedentary civilization,"[1] then we are and have long been a nation both advanced and sedentary.

An examination of the furniture industry is of particular significance for a study in the Racial Policies of American Industry Series in that so much of the industry and the black population of our country is in the South. Also of significance is the existence of a growing, low-visibility industry, made up of numerous small and generally nonunion plants, which is now being entered by large, highly visible conglomerates intent on restructuring the home furnishings industry.

Although the Negro has found employment in the furniture industry almost since its beginning, the last twenty-five years, and particularly the 1960s, have witnessed major employment gains for the Negro. It is therefore the purpose of this study to examine the current racial employment policy in the furniture industry within the context of the industry's structure and history. Major areas to be considered are the total employment picture of blue collar and white collar jobs, the effect of locational factors and civil rights legislation, equal employment problems, and future prospects for Negroes in the furniture industry.

To accomplish the objectives of this study much use has been made of census data, with additional information supplied by the Equal Employment Opportunity Commission and interviews with representatives of various furniture manufacturers in the United States.

---

1. J. L. Oliver, *The Development and Structure of the Furniture Industry* (New York: Pergamon Press, Inc., 1966), p. xiii.

CHAPTER II

The Furniture Industry

Furniture history in the United States began with the Englishmen who settled New England. It was they who "brought the trade of furniture making from old England and in these new environs were by 1675 making tables, chairs and chests of distinctly American design."[2] For the major portion of America's history, furniture making has been the work of individual skilled craftsmen, called cabinetmakers. It was not until the late 1800s, as the public became more prosperous and the demand for furniture increased, that cabinetmakers became unable to fill the public's need. The result was the development of factories able to mass produce furniture and the decline of the cabinetmaker's role. It was inevitable that "the makers of furniture, under the new regime, would be industrialists, not artists and craftsmen, and that the distributors, who were the necessary contact between the maker and the buyer, would be merchants and not connoisseurs."[3]

The furniture industry as it presently exists is an industry of many paradoxes. For example, it is an industry that is profitable, and apparently increasingly so, yet it has a failure rate four times the overall business average.[4] Once a highly skilled trade, it is now an industry heavily dependent on unskilled and semiskilled labor. Although its pay scale is among the lowest in all industry, it remains relatively ununionized. It is an industry employing a sizable work force, but the average size of each establishment is quite small. In general, it is an industry continuing to experience change.

2. Thomas H. Ormsbee, *Early American Furniture Makers* (New York: Tudor Publishing Co., 1930), p. 21.

3. A. P. Johnson and Marta K. Sironen, *Manual of the Furniture Arts and Crafts* (Grand Rapids, Michigan: A. P. Johnson Co., 1928), p. 604.

4. "Flaws in Furniture," *Duns Review*, 89 (May, 1967), p. 13.

THE PRODUCTION PROCESSES [5]

In some of the more advanced furniture manufacturing plants, Detroit-styled assembly lines are being adopted. Sophisticated techniques such as punch-type instructions for machines and optical scanners that trace cutting patterns electronically are beginning to be used. In addition, because quality woods are scarce and expensive, traditional furniture-grade wood and veneers are being replaced by new materials ranging from pressed panels made of wood chip to laminated plastic composites.[6] Although these innovations are making the manufacturing process more streamlined and efficient, they are not typical for the industry. For the industry as a whole, the production processes remain much more traditional, but nevertheless still able to service increasing consumer demands.

The typical process begins with the raw material, which is normally wood, especially hardwoods such as walnut, oak, maple, birch, beech, gum, and mahogany. Once the tree has been felled and transported to the saw mill, the logs are cut according to a set pattern to insure the maximum yield of high quality lumber. Work in these areas is normally performed by both unskilled and semiskilled labor.

When the rough-milling operation at the saw mill is completed the lumber must be kiln dried. It is important that the moisture level after kiln drying be that which will occur under normal conditions in the end product, or the furniture will have a tendency to split. The removing of moisture in a uniform way imparts a high degree of strength to the lumber and reduces the weight of the lumber by 40 to 60 percent, thereby making transportation more economical. Although the features of the kiln itself vary depending upon such factors as the location of the plant, the kind of lumber to be handled, and the quality of the ultimate product, kiln drying most often requires semiskilled workers.

The rough-milled lumber is taken from the dry-storage area to the finish milling and gluing operation where the lumber is

---

5. This entire section is based primarily on the following works: Julius Eisen, "A Survey of the Wood Household Furniture Industry, Past, Present and Future," (unpublished MBA thesis, University of Pennsylvania, 1960), pp. 59-73; and Johnson, *op. cit.*, pp. 375-462.

6. "Technology Restyles Furniture Business," *Business Week*, November 19, 1966, pp. 94-95.

cut into the size required for the furniture parts which will ultimately be produced. The lumber is then glued together to form "blanks" or "squares"—solid rectangles of lumber formed by joining numerous strips of wood by gluing. The gluing process, in addition to creating a more warp-resistant piece, is also a convenient means of obtaining maximum utilization of the various widths of lumber produced in the rough mill. The work level here is also semiskilled.

The machining operation is responsible for working the various-sized blanks into their final shape. This operation includes further sawing, shaping, routing, boring, planing, and sanding. At the conclusion of this operation, the parts for the finished piece of furniture have been produced. Because of inconsistencies in the quality of wood, relatively greater judgment is needed in this operation in order to make decisions which will insure maximum utilization of the raw material. Again, however, the work level is no higher than semiskilled.

A piece of furniture is produced through a number of assembly operations which are not highly mechanized. Because wood parts are often not of consistent dimension, much of the assembly work is done by hand to insure proper fit. If wood furniture is being assembled, the product is not only fitted together but also inspected, cleaned, finished, hand rubbed, waxed, and packaged for shipment. If upholstered furniture is being assembled, fabrics must be purchased, cut to size, sewn together, then joined with spring and frame assemblies either by a master upholsterer or by individuals performing highly specialized operations. From this point the product may be packaged and shipped.

The typical furniture manufacturer does not begin his operation any further back than the finish milling or kiln drying processes and some begin as late as the assembly phase. These latter manufacturers, particularly in metropolitan areas, purchase furniture parts from a firm specializing in the production of parts and merely assemble the furniture. Thus, the scope of the production process varies greatly throughout the industry.

INDUSTRIAL CHARACTERISTICS

Furniture, in the most general breakdown, can be divided into two major categories: upholstery and case goods (tables, cabinets, and chairs). Two-thirds of the industry's sales are in case goods, with the remainder in upholstered furniture.[7] The more common breakdown for purposes of analysis and the breakdown that will be utilized in this study is the federal government's Standard Industrial Classification (SIC) system. It should be noted that there is both a three-digit and a four-digit breakdown of the industry and its major segments. The four-digit breakdown is primarily applicable to the household furniture segment, where approximately 70 percent of industry employment is located. Here the major sectors are wood (2511) and upholstered (2512) household furniture.

Table 1 shows employment, payroll, capital expenditures, and other industrial data for the furniture and fixtures industry and major segments thereof for 1970. As can be seen, household furniture is the significant industry segment in terms of the industrial characteristics presented. A distant second place is occupied by the manufacturers of partitions and fixtures, i.e., a collection of establishments engaged in producing shelving, cabinets, display cases, prefabricated partitions, office and store fixtures, and other related fabricated products.

For all industry segments, but particularly for household furniture, the cost of materials seems to comprise a major portion of the value of shipments. The total industry figures show that materials represent approximately 46 percent, and labor 30 percent, of the value of shipments. For all manufacturing industries, materials and labor represent approximately 53 and 24 percent of the value of shipments, respectively.[8] As this indicates, the furniture industry is relatively labor intensive. Although the furniture industry is beginning to invest more in labor-saving equipment, it still remains considerably behind the industry average for new capital expenditures per employer. The capital expenditure per employee ratio for all manufacturing industries in 1970 was $1,136,[9] as compared to an average for the furniture industry of $559.

---

7. "Furniture Industry Review," Dominick & Dominick Research Dept., Nov. 19, 1970, p. 7.

8. U.S. Bureau of the Census, *Annual Survey of Manufactures: 1970, General Statistics for Industry Groups and Industries*, M70 (AS)-1, Preliminary Report, 1970, Table 1.

9. *Ibid.*

TABLE 1. *Furniture Industry*
Employment, Payroll, Capital Expenditures, and
Other Data by Standard Industrial Classification
1970

Industrial Characteristics	Total (SIC 25)	Household Furniture (SIC 251)	Office Furniture (SIC 252)	Public Building Furniture (SIC 253)	Partitions and Fixtures (SIC 254)	Misc. Furniture and Fixtures (SIC 259)
All Employees				Thousands of Employees		
All Employees	434.4	299.7	37.3	22.6	50.9	23.9
				Millions of Dollars		
Payroll	2,656.2	1,704.5	263.0	149.3	380.9	158.5
Value Added by Manufacture	4,842.2	3,093.3	523.3	252.5	682.3	290.8
Cost of Materials	4,149.8	2,859.1	340.9	214.0	510.5	225.3
Value of Shipments	8,967.4	5,932.8	876.2	461.7	1,188.3	508.4
Capital Expenditures, New	242.8	179.4	14.8	18.8	22.9	6.9

Source: U.S. Bureau of the Census, *Annual Survey of Manufactures: 1969, General Statistics for Industry Groups and Industries,* Preliminary Report, 1970, Table 1.

Industrial Structure

The furniture industry has traditionally been highly dispersed. As of the 1947 census only five other industries had more companies than the household furniture industry: saw mills and planing mills, bread and related products, newspapers, commercial printing, and dresses. An analysis of the concentration in 452 industries made by the Department of Commerce in 1947 showed that the upholstered furniture industry ranked 405th and the nonupholstered furniture industry ranked 446th.[10] The census for that year shows a total of 4,880 establishments[11] in the household furniture industry alone, while the entire furniture industry reported 7,687 establishments.[12]

In 1967, the size of the industry was estimated to be 5,350 separate companies with sales of $4 billion a year; however, only 27 of these firms had sales in excess of $10 million.[13] By 1969, the industry had reached sales of $4.8 billion (over $9 billion at retail). However, two-thirds of the more than 5,000 companies employed fewer than twenty people[14] and accounted for less than 8½ percent of industry shipments. The six largest companies accounted for approximately 12 to 13 percent of total sales, and only two of them had sales in excess of $100 million.[15] Table 2 sets forth statistics for the five major corporations in the industry as of 1969.[16]

---

10. Kenneth R. Davis, *Furniture Marketing* (Chapel Hill: University of North Carolina Press, 1957), pp. 43-46.

11. The Census of Manufactures defines establishment as "a single plant or factory . . . not necessarily identical with the business unit or company which may consist of one or more establishments."

12. U.S. Bureau of the Census, *Census of Manufactures: 1947*, Vol. II, *Statistics By Industry*, p. 293 and Table 1.

13. Thomas O'Hanlon, "5350 Companies: A Mixed-Up Furniture Industry," *Fortune*, February, 1967, p. 145.

14. There is a significant difference between the size of metal furniture and wood furniture establishments. Data from Table 4 of the *Census of Manufactures: 1967* (MC67[2]-25A and B) indicate that 67 percent of the wood household furniture establishments and 48 percent of the metal household furniture establishments employ fewer than twenty people. The corresponding figures for office furniture are 61 percent for wood and 36 percent for metal. Thus, it would appear that metal furniture establishments tend to be larger than their wood counterparts.

15. "Furniture Industry Review," *loc. cit.*

16. It should be pointed out that the majority of the furniture-producing companies, even companies with sales in the $80 to $90 million range, are unincorporated.

TABLE 2. *Furniture Industry*
The Five Largest Furniture Corporations, 1970

Company and 1970 Rank Among Industrial Corporations	Headquarters	Sales	Assets	Net Income	Invested Capital	Number of Employees	Net Income as a Percent of	
			Thousands of Dollars				Sales	Invested Capital
Bassett Furniture Industries (583)	Bassett, Va.	132,593	86,257	10,570	76,139	5,800	8.0	13.9
Kroehler Mfg. (657)	Naperville, Ill.	112,397	65,755	63 [a]	45,826	5,908	0.1	0.1
Lane (852)	Altavista, Va.	72,446	56,039	4,288	43,938	4,534	5.9	9.8
American Seating (889)	Grand Rapids, Mich.	67,375	57,502	1,198	30,815	2,600	1.8	3.9
Baumritter (937)	New York	62,199	51,816	2,890	33,364	3,400	4.6	8.7

Source: *Fortune*, Vol. 83, No. 6 (June, 1971), pp. 100-127.

[a] There was an extraordinary charge of at least 10 percent shown on the income statement.

Because the average furniture plant is relatively small, the industry does not have the public visibility that might be expected of a $5 billion industry. Consequently, relatively little public attention has been given to Negro employment in this trade.

Although the typical furniture-producing plant appears to be quite small, it will be shown later that the size will vary significantly among states, primarily because of the type of product being made and the extent of automation. In general, the states with the largest plants tend to produce medium and low price goods. In such plants specialization and mechanization can be more easily used. On the other hand, smaller plants tend to produce specialty products or merely assemble parts produced by others.[17]

A further reason for the large number of small plants in the industry is the relative ease of entering furniture manufacturing. This is most true in the upholstery operation, where little capital is needed. It has been estimated that it would currently require $1.00 of investment to produce $1.00 of case goods sales, but only $0.33 of investment to produce $1.00 of upholstery sales. This would explain why the majority of the 5,000 furniture companies are primarily local upholstery shops, although two-thirds of industry sales are in case goods. Of the five largest corporations in the United States only Kroehler Manufacturing is primarily a producer of upholstery rather than case goods.[18] Because the furniture industry does not have the high capital investment barrier found in other industries, it offers an opportunity to Negroes desiring to open businesses of their own.

In recent years the industry has experienced a slight decline in the number of companies. Instead of an industry decline, a reorganization of the industry is occurring. Firms are beginning to merge and conglomerates are beginning to buy into the industry.

The two largest companies in the industry have been quite active in the merger movement. As early as 1956 Kroehler began buying smaller concerns, particularly plants in the nonupholstery line, thereby diversifying its product line. This move was not as successful as hoped, and by 1970 Kroehler was phasing case goods out of operation.[19] Bassett Furniture Industries, in ad-

---

17. Eisen, *op. cit.*, p. 82.

18. "Furniture Industry Review," *op. cit.*, p. 7.

19. "Analyst Peers into Crystal Ball and Sights Six Smashing Stocks," *Home Furnishings Daily*, December 9, 1970, p. 13.

dition to continuing to supply capital to enable relatives and favored employees to start their own plants, has also begun acquiring additional companies.[20] Merger activity has not been limited to the largest companies, as companies with sales in the $20 to $30 million range have also been quite active.[21]

The traditional fragmentation and high profitability of the industry have attracted an increasing number of outsiders. Companies such as Burlington Industries, Mohasco Corporation, U. S. Plywood-Champion Paper, Armstrong Cork, Magnavox, Mead Corporation, Massey-Ferguson, Dolly Madison, Sequoyah Industries, and RCA have been among those to respond. It has not been unusual for some of these acquiring companies to pay as much as twenty-six times earnings—a price earning multiple considerably higher than those usually paid for consumer goods companies.[22]

Among the conglomerates entering the furniture industry, many are companies already involved in various segments of the home-furnishings industry, particularly the carpet industry. Companies such as Armstrong Cork, Burlington Industries, and Mohasco Industries, already established in the carpet industry, are moving into the furniture industry so as to offer the consumer completely integrated interiors or home-furnishings packages.[23]

The rationale for many of the recent acquisitions is that

furniture should not be treated as a separate consumer entity but as the backbone of the $12-billion retail home-furnishing industry. Companies with this approach plan to add carpet, textile, and accessory manufacturers to their furniture acquisitions. They aim to offer the consumer a coordinated package of products backed by national distribution and brand name advertising. Says one manufacturer: "We are seeing the creation of an entirely new consumer industry." [24]

Thus, the expansionist activity of these conglomerates seems to be directed toward the emergence of home-center markets where

20. O'Hanlon, *op. cit.*, p. 147.

21. Industry data supplied by the Armstrong Cork Company's Marketing Research Library, January 25, 1971.

22. Isadore Barmash, "Home Furnishings Industry Goes Big Time," *New York Times*, May 16, 1971, p. 2f.

23. See Robert W. Kirk, *The Carpet Industry*, Industrial Research Reports, Miscellaneous Series, Report No. 17 (Philadelphia: Industrial Research Unit, Wharton School, University of Pennsylvania, 1970), pp. 20-30.

24. O'Hanlon, *op. cit.*, p. 147.

the consumer can furnish his home by purchasing the various elements in complete design packages.[25]

It is predicted that continued acquisitions and consolidations will occur. One furniture executive has gone on record as believing that "within ten or fifteen years fifty companies will account for 90 percent of the volume in furniture. A company with $300 million in sales will not be unusual." [26]

Of the 5,350 companies making up the industry in 1967, only 18 were publicly owned, and the majority of the remaining firms were family owned. Family ownership is particularly evident in the South. With the exception of a few companies such as Drexel Enterprises and Thomasville Furniture Industries, the southern firms are still controlled or managed by the men who founded them or by their descendants.[27]

Although a considerable portion of the industry is being affected by mergers and the entry of conglomerates, none of the largest firms have been absorbed. Table 3 reveals one possible reason for this situation: because of the small amount of stock it would appear difficult for an outside party to gain control. In fact, at present Kroehler is the only firm engaged primarily as a furniture producer that is listed on the New York Stock Exchange; and only four companies—Aberdeen, Brody, General Interiors, and RBI—are listed on the American Stock Exchange.

The present fragmentized nature of the industry presents both advantages and disadvantages for the Negro. If he desires to open his own production facility the ease of entry into the industry is advantageous, particularly in the area of upholstered furniture. On the other hand, it is unlikely that government pressure would be directed at promoting greater employment opportunities within so many small companies when there are much larger companies in other industries. The entry of conglomerates and the merger movement within the industry should change this situation somewhat. The conglomerates, which are usually large employers, have a public image to maintain, and as small companies merge and become more visible, they too will develop an awareness of their public image and feel the pressure to be known as an equal opportunity employer.

---

25. "Packages Seen Half of '80 Sales," *Home Furnishings Daily*, April 8, 1971, p. 8.

26. O'Hanlon, *op. cit.*, p. 182.

27. *Ibid.*, pp. 145-147 and Barmash, *op. cit.*, p. 2f.

TABLE 3. *Furniture Industry*
Stock Structure of Major Furniture Manufacturers, 1970

Company	Shares Outstanding	Estimated Float (Shares)	Dollar Value of Float
Kroehler	1,289,000	500,000	8,500,000
Baumritter	1,200,000	600,000	19,800,000
Bassett	6,012,000	1,000,000	33,000,000
American	2,679,000	2,000,000	10,000,000
Lane	2,478,000	750,000	22,500,000
Henredon	1,327,500	800,000	25,600,000
Total	14,985,500		119,400,000

Source: "Furniture Industry Review," Dominick & Dominick Research Department, November 19, 1970, p. 17.

Industrial Growth

Since 1947 the furniture industry has experienced constant expansion in terms of total establishments and value added (Table 4). In recent years, this growth has been reflected in virtually all areas of the industry. Table 5 shows that from 1963 to 1969 there has been a 7.69 percent annual increase in dollar volume of business for the two major segments of the industry—household, and office and public building furniture. The rate of increase has been higher for the office and public building segment—10.20 percent, as opposed to 6.98 percent for the household segment. However, the household segment continues to dominate in dollar volume. It is expected that the growth rate in the industry will continue at approximately the same pace at least through 1973.

Although the growth rate of office furniture surpasses that of household furniture, the latter is not only the major segment in terms of total Negro employment, but is also the segment with the greatest percentage increase in Negro employment since 1964. Equal Employment Opportunity Commission data for 1964 and 1969 show that the percentage of Negroes employed in the office furniture segment has increased from 5.4 percent to 9.2

TABLE 4. *Furniture Industry*
The Number of Establishments and Value Added by Region
1947-1967

Year	UNITED STATES [a]		NORTHEAST		NORTH CENTRAL		SOUTH		WEST	
	Number of Establish-ments	Value Added (in thou-sands)	Number of Establish-ments	Value Added (in thou-sands)	Number of Establish-ments	Value Added (in thou-sands)	Number of Establish-ments	Value Added (in thou-sands)	Number of Establish-ments	Value Added (in thou-sands)
1967	10,008	4,169,500	2,960	922,000	2,157	1,246,400	2,820	1,524,200	2,071	476,700
1963	10,478	3,068,287	3,229	717,931	2,305	936,829	2,799	1,030,247	2,146	389,059
1958	10,160	2,349,488	3,284	606,579	2,333	782,680	2,666	686,863	1,877	269,298
1954	10,273	1,966,410	3,532	539,262	2,423	738,302	2,515	494,603	1,803	194,239
1947	n.a.	1,346,277	n.a.	366,045	n.a.	545,090	n.a.	309,239	n.a.	125,903

Source: U.S. Bureau of the Census, *Census of Manufactures: 1954, 1958, 1963, 1967*, Table 2.

[a] Figures given for regions do not add to U.S. total.

TABLE 5. Furniture Industry

Household and Office and Public Building Furniture Production, 1963-1967

(Thousands of Dollars)

	Grand Total	HOUSEHOLD					OFFICE AND PUBLIC BUILDINGS				
		Wood	Upholstered	Metal	Other Household	Total Household	Office Wood	Office Metal	Public Bldg. and Rel. Furn.	Other Furn. and Fixtures	Total Office
1963	4,182,636	1,759,283	958,989	507,728	46,867	3,272,867	100,889	358,062	263,291	138,027	859,769
1964	4,467,596	1,911,256	1,026,892	546,526	51,922	3,536,596	109,152	394,952	284,883	142,213	981,000 a
1965	4,878,127	2,063,783	1,153,197	548,129	65,145	3,830,204	123,554	456,649	309,258	158,462	1,047,923
1966	5,375,744	2,262,214	1,233,598	579,191	70,872	4,145,870	138,079	571,669	340,337	179,789	1,229,874
1967	5,484,832	2,299,000	1,242,100	579,500	78,700	4,199,300	158,700	584,200	355,652 (E)	186,980 (E)	1,285,532
Est. 1968	5,984,270	2,525,000	1,353,000	631,000	77,970	4,586,970	169,600	645,000	382,700	200,000	1,397,300
Est. 1969	6,281,200	2,646,000	1,411,000	641,000	81,000	4,779,000	184,200	700,000	404,000	214,000	1,502,200
1963-1968 Gain	44.31%	43.52%	41.09%	24.28%	66.36%	40.15%	68.94%	80.14%	45.35%	44.90%	62.52%
Yearly Gain Compounded	7.69%	7.49%	7.18%	4.44%	10.72%	6.98%	11.06%	12.49%	7.77%	7.79%	10.20%
Est. 1973	8,016,800	3,400,000	1,800,000	755,000	125,000	6,080,000	242,400	926,200	502,800	265,400	1,986,800
1968-1973 Gain	33.96%	34.65%	33.04%	19.65%	60.32%	32.55%	42.92%	43.60%	31.38%	32.70%	38.61%
Yearly Gain Compounded	6.02%	6.18%	5.88%	3.65%	9.90%	5.80%	7.40%	7.61%	5.61%	5.82%	6.75%

Source: Armstrong Cork Company Marketing Research Library, "Industry Data," p. A-1.

a Segments for Office and Public Buildings, 1964, do not add to total given in source.

percent, or a 70.4 percent increase, while household furniture has increased from 8.2 percent to 15.1 percent, or an 84.2 percent increase.[28]

Although many of the companies in the industry have often been criticized as being "insignificant in size, inbred in management, inefficient in production, and inherently opposed to technological change," [29] it appears that the situation is improving. Since 1962, refinements of the production line, such as more automation, use of sophisticated inventory techniques, and use of wood substitutes have increased productivity (Table 6). Over the same period of time the industry's average manufacturing costs per $100 of sales has declined by 3.9 percent (Table 7).

The growth of the past appears likely to continue into the future. For the next four to five years, rising income levels and other favorable demographic factors such as the number of family formations, size of the various age groups, rate of residential construction, availability of credit, and population mobility, should combine to enable the furniture industry to grow at an estimated annual rate of at least 8 percent.[30]

In addition, the development of new products and processes will also have a favorable effect. Foremost among these changes is the increasing use of plastics. In 1968 the total use of plastics in the furniture industry was up 21 percent over the previous year. With the increasing cost of wood and the increasing interest in contemporary plastic designs, it is estimated that by 1975 plastic in furniture parts will attain the 700 million-pound-a-year level, representing a 25 percent penetration of the total home-furnishings market. One furniture manufacturing executive has predicted that within ten years plastics will capture at least 80 percent of the mass furniture market.[31]

Although there are potential problems on the horizon, such as increasing imports of furniture and transportation problems, it seems likely that the industry is on the threshold of major favorable changes as new companies, products, processes, materials, and marketing approaches make their presence felt. These changes should more than compensate for the problems

28. Data in author's possession.

29. *O'Hanlon, op. cit.,* p. 145.

30. "Furniture Industry Review," *op. cit.,* p. 12.

31. "Plastics Make Themselves at Home," *Business Week,* February 8, 1969, pp. 50-52.

TABLE 6. *Furniture Industry*
Productivity Trends, 1962-1970

	Case Goods	Upholstered	All Reporting Plants
1970	$16,635	$19,974	$18,254
1969	15,726	19,970	17,556
1968	15,339	19,516	17,180
1967	15,203	18,706	16,301
1966	15,051	18,510	16,171
1965	13,760	16,885	14,966
1964	13,627	14,586	14,265
1963	13,608	15,402	14,745
1962	12,744	15,353	13,623

Sources: "Furniture Industry Review," Dominick & Dominick Research Dept.,
Nov. 19, 1970, p. 12, and *Home Furnishings Daily*, Oct. 19, 1971.

TABLE 7. *Furniture Industry*
Average Production Cost Trend Per $100 of Sales, 1962-1969

	Material	Percent of Total	Direct Labor	Percent of Total	Factory Overhead	Percent of Total	Total
1969	$37.92	50.7	$18.08	24.2	$18.83	25.2	$74.83
1968	36.71	49.1	18.88	25.3	19.15	25.6	74.74
1967	38.71	51.0	18.92	24.8	18.24	24.1	75.87
1966	39.70	52.2	18.60	24.5	17.66	23.2	75.96
1965	39.95	52.2	18.85	24.8	17.33	22.8	76.13
1964	39.75	51.8	18.54	24.2	18.43	24.0	76.72
1963	41.66	53.9	17.96	23.3	17.63	22.8	77.23
1962	42.32	54.3	18.36	23.6	17.22	22.1	77.89

Source: "Furniture Industry Review," Dominick & Dominick Research Dept.,
Nov. 19, 1970, p. 11.

likely to arise. The Department of Commerce has predicted that manufacturers' shipments of household furniture alone should reach $8.0 billion by 1975 (an increase of more than 7 percent each year) and $10.8 billion by 1980.[32]

Because of its continuing growth, particularly in terms of employment, the furniture industry appears, for the time being, to be one industry in which the Negro, as well as other job seekers, can expect increasing employment opportunities. One drawback that may be felt in the long run is the gradual reduction in the percentage of blue collar workers. With increasing mechanization it can be anticipated that the reduction may continue and eventually reach the point where employment levels remain fairly constant or even decrease as output increases. This development would greatly affect Negro employment, since blacks are almost completely concentrated in blue collar jobs.

Customer Orientation

Furniture is a product familiar to everyone, but unlike most consumer products, few people associate the product with the manufacturer's name. Until recently consumer advertising was delegated to the retailer, and the manufacturer concentrated on convincing the retailer to carry his product. The lack of direct consumer orientation may have contributed to the industry's remoteness from social problems.

In recent years, however, two marketing trends are emerging which may increase consumer awareness of manufacturers. First, larger companies have begun advertising, some stressing price and style and a few emphasizing their trade names and the quality of their product. Second, there is the emergence of manufacturers offering coordinated packages. These will be offered as a unit to the retailer and advertised in that manner.[33] These trends could bring about much greater public visibility of furniture manufacturers and, consequently, greater public attention to their racial employment practices.

Industrial Location

The geographical location of the furniture industry has historically been a matter of shifting regions of concentration.

---

32. U.S. Department of Commerce, *U.S. Industrial Outlook 1972,* (Washington: U.S. Government Printing Office, 1972), p. 110.

33. "Furniture Industry Review," *op. cit.,* pp. 9-10.

From the early days of the industry until the middle of the nineteenth century, the industry was almost solely located in the New England and Middle Atlantic areas. As the population moved westward, so did the industry. By 1850 the industry had begun moving to take advantage of the available supply of lumber and to service the western markets that could not be economically serviced by eastern manufacturers. The result was a new concentration of the industry in the Midwest, particularly in the Cincinnati and Grand Rapids areas.

As industry began moving to the South in the early 1900s and particularly in the post-World War I period, so did the furniture industry. The availability of lumber was again a major impetus, but in addition, the abundant supply of low-cost labor was appealing to an industry that was becoming increasingly dependent on unskilled and semiskilled labor. Because of these two factors and an increasing southern market for furniture, the industry has continued to move to the South. By 1962, 35.4 percent of the furniture industry in the United States was located in the South.[34] Key southern furniture centers have now developed in the areas surrounding High Point, North Carolina; Morristown, Tennessee, and Fort Smith, Arkansas. In addition to the current southern movement of the furniture industry, there has also been a lesser but constant movement to the West Coast, where there is an expanding market.

As the South and West have recorded gains in furniture employment, the remaining regions, particularly the North Central, have not been as fortunate. For example, the states of Michigan and Illinois, where the industry once tended to concentrate, led all states in the number of furniture jobs lost between 1929 and 1954—approximately 13,000 each.[35] From 1954 to 1966 Michigan experienced a further decline of 1,215 jobs, or 5.8 percent, while Illinois remained relatively stable.[36] The industry decline in Michigan as well as in the entire North

---

34. F. Ray Marshall, *Labor in the South* (Cambridge, Mass.: Harvard University Press, 1967), p. 317.

35. Victor R. Fuchs, *Changes in the Location of Manufacturing in the United States Since 1929* (New Haven: Yale University Press, 1962), p. 245.

36. U.S. Bureau of the Census, *Annual Survey of Manufactures: 1966, Statistics for States, Standard Metropolitan Statistical Areas and Large Industrial Counties*, M66 (AS)-7.3, Table 3.

Central region seems due primarily to the declining household furniture industry of that region.

In general, the furniture industry's localization has historically been dependent upon lumber supply, labor supply, and the existence of markets. In recent years, the last two factors appear to be the more important.[37]

Table 4 shows that the furniture industry, in terms of the number of establishments, is more heavily concentrated in the Northeast. However, when the industry is considered in terms of value added by manufacture, the Northeast region drops to a distant third place behind the South and the North Central regions. In addition, Table 8 shows that in terms of total employment, the industry is heavily concentrated in the South, followed distantly by the North Central and Northeast regions. The differences between establishment concentration, employment, and value concentration are attributable to the existence of numerous small facilities in the Northeast, many producing specialty products, while the South, and to a lesser extent the North Central region, tend to have larger, more automated facilities producing more standard products.

Although the industry appears to be well represented in all of the major geographical regions, within these regions a few states account for a major portion of the industry. In 1970, North Carolina, California, New York, Pennsylvania, Illinois, and Virginia accounted for almost half of the industry's value added, value of shipments, and employment. North Carolina alone accounted for 13.2 percent of value added, 13.1 percent of industry shipments, and 15.4 percent of employment.[38] The heavy concentration of the industry in the North Carolina area is shown further by the fact that twenty-three of the top thirty furniture manufacturers are located in a 150-mile belt stretching from Bassett, Virginia to Lenoir, North Carolina.[39]

As mentioned earlier, the location of the industry has always been dependent upon the availability of raw materials, a supply of low-cost labor, and the existence of markets. This explains

---

37. George L. Leffler and Mary V. Brown, "Trends in the Furniture Industry," Pennsylvania State College, Bureau of Business Research, Bulletin No. 18, 1944, pp. 1-2.

38. U.S. Bureau of the Census, *Annual Survey of Manufactures: 1970, Statistics for Divisions and States*, M70 (AS)-6.2, 6.3, 6.5, 6.9.

39. O'Hanlon, *op. cit.*, p. 147.

TABLE 8. *Furniture Industry
Employment by Region, 1969*

Region	Total Employees		Production Employees	
	Number	Percent	Number	Percent
United States [a]	455,600	100.0	381,500	100.0
Northeast	95,800	21.0	79,800	20.9
North Central	117,600	25.8	94,100	24.7
South	192,500	42.3	166,500	43.6
West	49,400	10.9	41,000	10.8

Sources: U.S. Bureau of the Census, *Annual Survey of Manufactures: 1969,
General Statistics for Industry Groups and Industries*, M69 (AS)-1,
Table 1, and *Statistics for States, Standard Metropolitan Statistical
Areas, Large Industrial Counties and Selected Cities*, M69 (AS)
6.1-6.9, Table 2.

[a] Sections do not add to United States total because of statistical inaccuracies
in state reporting techniques.

the concentration of the industry in such diverse states as New
York, where the location tends to be large metropolitan areas,
and North Carolina, where the location is in the more rural
portions of the state.[40] Even though the industry as a whole
appears to be well represented in most of the major national
regions, this is not the case for various segments of the industry. In terms of employment, the South is the dominant region
for the wood, upholstery, and metal household furniture segments, as well as the mattresses and springs segment. The
North Central region has a slight edge over other regions in
wood and metal office furniture, public building furniture, metal
partitions and fixtures, venetian blinds and shades, and miscellaneous furniture and fixtures. The Northeast has only a slight
lead in the remaining two areas, miscellaneous household furniture and wood partitions and fixtures. Although the West is
not a dominant region in any of the above segments, the state

40. According to the 1960 Census 73.3 percent of New York's furniture
industry is located in standard metropolitan areas of 250,000 population or more, while 57.6 percent is located in New York City. For North
Carolina only 17.0 percent of the furniture industry's employment is
located in standard metropolitan areas of 100,000 population or more.

of California leads all other states in employment in **springs** and mattresses and public building furniture.[41]

Negro employment has been aided considerably by the current geographical concentration of the industry. First, the industry is becoming increasingly concentrated in the South, where the majority of Negroes reside. Second, because of their production methods, the majority of the plants in the South have less need for skilled labor. The result is the elimination of some employment barriers that might exist in other regions.

MANPOWER

Employment in the furniture industry, except during short-term fluctuations in the economy, has continued to increase. Between 1947 and 1970 employment increased from 336 million to 460 million. This growth is normally attributed to the corresponding increase in consumer-disposable income. As income has risen, the amount that the consumer has been willing to spend on furniture has also risen. Other factors that have contributed to the growth are the increasing number of family formations and increases in the size of the various furniture-buying age groups within the population.[42]

Although the furniture industry accounts for less than 3 percent of total industry employment, it represents a significant source of employment in the South, particularly in states such as North Carolina, Virginia, Arkansas, Tennessee, and Mississippi. In each of these states, furniture is one of the top seven industries in terms of employment, and except for Tennessee, one of the top eight industries in terms of total wages and value added by manufacture.[43]

As the furniture industry has grown and become more concentrated in the South, an increasing percentage of Negroes have been employed. The 1960 census reported total Negro employment in the industry as being 27,938, or 7.4 percent of

41. U.S. Bureau of the Census, *Census of Manufactures, 1967*, Industry Series: *Office, Public Building and Miscellaneous Furniture; Office and Store Fixtures*, MC67(2)-25B Table 2, and Industry Series: *Household Furniture*, MC67(2)-25A, Table 2.

42. "Furniture Industry Review," *op. cit.*, p. 2.

43. U.S. Bureau of the Census, *Annual Survey of Manufactures: 1966, Statistics for States, Standard Metropolitan Statistical Areas and Large Industrial Counties*, M66 (AS)-7.5-7.7, Table 3.

the work force.[44] By 1969, data from the Equal Employment Opportunity Commission estimated the percentage to have risen to approximately 13.4 percent.[45] If the industry continues to grow, as is projected, it could become increasingly important as a source of Negro employment.

Occupational Distribution

Employment in the furniture industry is heavily concentrated in blue collar jobs. Although the ratio of blue collar workers to all employees has declined during the past quarter of a century, it still represents, as of 1970, 82.4 percent of total employment in the industry (Table 9).

Although there are some skilled jobs in furniture manufacturing, such as upholstering or carving, the trend in recent years has been away from craft jobs, and toward a more mechanized means of production.[46] The result has been a reduction in both the overall need for skilled labor and the percentage of employees involved in production work. At present, however, the industry does not resemble a mass-production industry, and the overall quality of labor is semiskilled.

When examined in closer detail, the typical employee in a furniture establishment is likely to be either an operative or a laborer (Table 10). Although Table 10 covers only 1,139 establishments in the industry, it does give a representative view of the occupational distribution as of 1969.

The relative lack of professionals in white collar jobs is explained by the lack of research and development and original design work done by most furniture establishments. As a group, professionals, technicians, and sales workers account for only 4.5 percent of total employment; this combined category accounts for less employment than does any other one category, except service workers. According to Kenneth R. Davis, the furniture industry needs no skills so unique that the supply is restricted.

Any shortages that might develop would be among key engineering, designing and promotion personnel, but even these skills can be bought in the management personnel market without too much difficulty. Much

---

44. See Chapter III, Table 16.

45. Data in author's possession. Percentage is based on a survey of 1,139 establishments.

46. Davis, *op. cit.*, p. 48.

TABLE 9. *Furniture Industry*
Total and Production Worker Employment
1947-1970

Year	All Employees	Production Workers	Percent of All Employees
		(Thousands)	
1947	336	296	88.1
1948	346	304	87.9
1949	317	274	86.4
1950	364	317	87.1
1951	357.2	307.1	86.0
1952	357.1	305.6	85.6
1953	369.9	315.9	85.4
1954	341.9	287.7	84.1
1955	363.8	307.0	84.4
1956	375.5	315.5	84.0
1957	374.3	313.0	83.6
1958	360.8	298.7	82.8
1959	385.0	321.0	83.4
1960	383.0	318.5	83.2
1961	367.5	303.9	82.7
1962	385.1	319.6	83.0
1963	389.9	324.1	83.1
1964	405.9	337.0	83.0
1965	430.7	357.4	83.0
1966	461.5	382.5	82.9
1967	455.4	374.9	82.3
1968	471.6	389.5	82.6
1969	483.5	401.2	83.0
1970	459.9	378.9	82.4

Sources: U.S. Bureau of Labor Statistics, *Employment and Earnings, United States, 1909-1970*, Bulletin 1312-7, pp. 59-60, and *Employment and Earnings*, March 1971, Table B-2.

TABLE 10. *Furniture Industry*
Distribution of Employment by Occupational Group
1,139 Establishments
United States, 1969

Occupational Group	Employees	Percent of Total
Officials and managers	17,925	6.4
Professionals	2,894	1.0
Technicians	3,810	1.4
Sales workers	5,802	2.1
Office and clerical workers	20,480	7.4
Total white collar	50,911	18.3
Craftsmen	48,205	17.4
Operatives	107,853	38.8
Laborers	66,534	23.9
Service workers	4,393	1.6
Total blue collar	226,985	81.7
Total	277,896	100.0

Source: Appendix Table A-4.

has been said and written about the inability of the furniture industry to attract the necessary managerial talents, and curricula have been established at the state universities of Michigan and North Carolina to train personnel for this industry. It is probably true, however, that factors other than training explain the long run shortcomings that may exist in the industry's management. One of these factors is "inbreeding." [47]

There is a significant variation within the furniture industry in regard to the blue collar vs. white collar breakdown. Table 11 shows that the major segment of the industry, household furniture, has 15.6 percent of its work force in white collar jobs, and 84.4 percent in blue collar jobs. The fastest growing segment of the industry, office furniture, shows a breakdown

47. *Ibid.*, p. 52.

TABLE 11. *Furniture Industry
Distribution of Employment by Occupational Group
Household Furniture Manufacturers and Office
Furniture Manufacturers, 1969*

Occupational Group	Household Furniture[a] Employees		Office Furniture[a] Employees	
	Number	Percent	Number	Percent
Officials and managers	12,058	6.0	2,223	6.9
Professionals	1,494	0.8	439	1.4
Technicians	1,671	0.8	643	2.0
Sales workers	3,203	1.6	1,030	3.2
Office and clerical workers	12,828	6.4	2,997	9.3
Total white collar	31,254	15.6	7,332	22.8
Craftsmen	37,322	18.6	3,774	11.8
Operatives	78,191	39.1	14,314	44.6
Laborers	50,095	25.0	6,265	19.5
Service workers	3,354	1.7	414	1.3
Total blue collar	168,962	84.4	24,767	77.2
Total	200,216	100.0	32,099	100.0

Source: U.S. Equal Employment Opportunity Commission.

[a] Household Furniture: 808 establishments; Office Furniture: 100 establishments.

of 22.8 percent and 77.2 percent, respectively. Among white collar jobs, all occupational groups show higher percentages in the office furniture segment than in household furniture. Among blue collar workers, the office furniture breakdown shows a lower percentage in all major occupational categories but operatives. Operatives comprise 44.6 percent of the office furniture work force, although the household furniture segment is only 39.1 percent operatives. The distinction here is primarily due to the nature of the material being used in production. The most often used material for office furniture is metal, which is more easily adapted to an assembly line operation than is wood, the prime material for household furniture. The use of wood requires a greater number of craftsmen.

With the level of employment continuing to increase in the furniture industry and with the heavy concentration of jobs in the unskilled and semiskilled categories, there should be few barriers for Negroes desiring to enter the industry. The situation is quite different when only white collar jobs are under consideration. Because of the relative lack of jobs in the white collar categories and the tendency for family ownership and management of companies, the prospects for employment would not appear good for Negroes or for anyone outside the family. This is particularly true for the higher level jobs.

Female Employment

The furniture industry began employing women prior to the turn of the century. As of 1880 the census for that year reported that women made up over 3 percent of the work force and were found in job categories ranging from "operatives, skilled and unskilled" to "officers, firm members, and clerks." In these categories, however, the rate of compensation was 60.5 percent and 55.3 percent of that of their male counterparts.[48]

The major increases in employment levels for women came during World Wars I and II. Since World War II, the level of female employment has increased steadily. Table 12 shows that from 1965 to 1970 the proportion of female employment has risen 6 percentage points, or greater than 1 percentage point a year, to a level of 24.3 percent of total employment.[49] As the table further shows, there is a significant difference between various segments of the industry. While partitions and fixtures has a work force which is only 11.9 percent female, upholstered household furniture, and other furniture and fixtures employ 30.4 percent and 28.8 percent, respectively. As

---

48. *Report on Manufacturing Industries in the United States at the Eleventh Census: 1890*, Part I, 1893, pp. 18-21.

49. This compares to increases of 2, 2, and 1 percentage points for all manufacturers, durable manufacturers, and nondurable manufacturers, respectively. The greatest increases in the employment of women have occurred in furniture, the sector with the lowest wage structure. (*Employment and Earnings*, March 1971, Table B-3, and U.S. Bureau of Labor Statistics, *Employment and Earnings, United States, 1909-1970*, Bulletin 1312-7).

TABLE 12. *Furniture Industry*
Total and Female Employment by Standard
Industrial Classification, 1965 and 1970

Industry Group	All Employees		Female		Percent Female	
	1965	1970	1965	1970	1965	1970
	(Thousands)					
Furniture and Fixtures (SIC 25)	430.7	459.9	77.5	111.9	18.0	24.3
Household Furniture (SIC 251)	309.2	320.8	58.0	85.3	18.8	26.6
Wood Household Furniture (SIC 2511)	160.5	160.3	22.9	37.8	14.3	23.6
Upholstered Household Furniture (SIC 2512)	78.4	85.8	18.8	26.1	24.0	30.4
Mattresses and Bedsprings (SIC 2515)	36.3	37.6	9.8	10.9	27.0	29.0
Office Furniture (SIC 252)	30.2	37.3	3.9	6.1	12.9	16.4
Partitions and Fixtures (SIC 254)	43.5	51.4	3.9	6.1	9.0	11.9
Other Furniture and Fixtures (SIC 253,9)	47.8	50.4	11.8	14.5	24.7	28.8

Sources: *Employment and Earnings*, March 1971, Tables B-2 and B-3, and U.S. Bureau of Labor Statistics, *Employment and Earnings, United States, 1909-1970*, Bulletin 1312-7, pp. 59-71.

of 1969, 75.9 percent of the female work force for the entire industry was employed in blue collar jobs and was fairly equally distributed between the categories of operatives and laborers. Of the female white collar workers, over 90 percent were in the category of office and clerical workers, and only 2.2 percent of the entire female work force was found in the combined categories of managers, professionals, technicians, and sales workers.[50]

The employment of Negro women in the furniture industry dates back almost as far as the employment of white women, but in considerably smaller numbers. Not until the World War II era were Negro women employed in any significant numbers. By 1960 the number of Negro women in the industry had risen to 4,219, or approximately 1.1 percent of the furniture work

50. Data in author's possession.

force. Among Negro women in the industry in 1969, 96.5 percent were employed in blue collar jobs, and the remaining 3.5 percent were employed almost solely as office and clerical workers.[51]

Earnings and Hours

An employee working for a furniture-producing company is likely to be among the lowest-paid employees of all industry. The average weekly earnings and average hourly earnings are well below the average for all manufacturing industries, as well as for the durable and nondurable segments of industry (see Table 13). As of 1970, the wages paid to furniture employees were the lowest for all manufacturers of durable products, and only three nondurable industries—textile-mill products, apparel and related products, and leather and leather products—paid lower rates.[52] Within the furniture industry, household furniture, which employs 70 percent of all industry employees, pays significantly lower rates than any other segment. Furthermore, within the household furniture segment, wood household furniture, which employs 50 percent of all household employees, or 35 percent of all industry employees, pays more than $10 a week less than any other sector within the industry. In addition, although the average number of hours worked per week is more comparable to industry averages, only one other durable goods industry classification, miscellaneous manufacturing, reported fewer hours worked.

The impetus for the industry's movement to the South—relatively lower wages—continues to be significant (see Table 14). As of 1969, the average hourly rate paid by southern furniture manufacturers was $2.21, compared to a national average of $2.57. The Northeast paid the next lowest rate, which was $0.50 an hour more than the southern average. The household furniture segment also shows a significant variation, as the southern rate of $2.19 an hour is $0.36 less than the next lowest region. In general, only in the South were rates sometimes below $2.25 an hour, whereas for various industry segments, the North Central states and the West sometimes paid rates greater than $3.50 per hour.

---

51. *Ibid.*

52. *Employment and Earnings*, March 1971, Table C-2.

TABLE 13. *Furniture and All Manufacturing Industries
Earnings and Hours Worked
Production (Nonsupervisory) Workers, 1970*

Industry	Average Weekly Earnings	Average Hourly Earnings	Average Weekly Hours
All manufacturing	$133.73	$3.36	39.8
Durable goods	143.47	3.56	40.3
Nondurable goods	120.43	3.08	39.1
Furniture and fixtures	108.58	2.77	39.2
Household furniture	101.79	2.61	39.0
Wood household furniture	96.14	2.44	39.4
Upholstered household furniture	107.52	2.80	38.4
Mattresses and bedsprings	110.97	2.86	38.8
Office furniture	123.86	3.12	39.7
Partitions and fixtures	134.13	3.37	39.8
Other furniture and fixtures	117.32	2.97	39.5

Source: *Employment and Earnings*, March 1971, Table C-2.

The relative lack of unionism in the industry, the lack of skills and educational requirements for employment, the heavy concentration of the industry in the South, and the increasing employment of Negroes and women all help to explain the low rates that continue to be paid in the industry. Particularly in the South, as new industry moves in, many white men are able to move to better-paying jobs. As a result, the furniture industry has provided opportunities for women and Negroes by turning to them as a source of employment. As in the textile industry, the lack of required skills has been an advantage in increasing the level of Negro employment in the furniture industry.[53]

53. Richard L. Rowan, "The Negro In The Textile Industry," *Negro Employment in Southern Industry*, Studies of Negro Employment, Vol. IV (Philadelphia: Industrial Research Unit, Wharton School, University of Pennsylvania, 1970), pp. 26-29.

TABLE 14. *Furniture Industry*

Average Hourly Earnings [a] of Production Workers by Standard Industrial Classification Groups United States and Regions, 1969

Region	Furniture & Fixtures (SIC 25)	Household Furniture (SIC 251)	Office Furniture (SIC 252)	Public Building Furniture (SIC 253)	Partitions and Fixtures (SIC 254)	Miscellaneous Furniture & Fixtures (SIC 259)
United States	2.57	2.41	3.11	2.58	3.11	2.84
Northeast	2.71	2.55	2.84	n.a.	3.15	2.60
North Central	2.92	2.62	3.87	2.87	3.12	3.66
South	2.21	2.19	2.29	2.06	2.35	2.60
West	3.15	2.89	n.a.	3.74	4.37	n.a.

Sources: U.S. Bureau of the Census, *Annual Survey of Manufactures: 1969, General Statistics for Industry Groups and Industries*, M69 (AS) -1, Table 1, and *Statistics for States, Standard Metropolitan Statistical Areas, Large Industrial Counties and Selected Cities*, M69 (AS) 6.1-6.9, Table 2.

[a] **Average Hourly Earnings = Wages ÷ Man-hours.**

Turnover

Table 15 presents a description of the furniture industry's turnover experience for two contrasting years. The years 1958 and 1968 were chosen since they reflect two different economic conditions in the nation: 1958 was a recession year with high unemployment, whereas 1968 was a year of economic growth and full employment.

The traditionally low wages paid by the furniture industry seem to account in a large measure for the high turnover rate experienced by the industry. The correlation between wages and turnover seems particularly strong when the household furniture segment is contrasted to a higher-paying segment, such as office furniture. In virtually all categories, for both years, the experience of household furniture is considerably worse than that of office furniture, with the wood household furniture sector showing the poorest performance.

In 1968 the furniture industry had the second highest quit rate among all manufacturers. Only the lumber industry, with a rate of 4.2 quits per 100 employees, exceeded the 4.1 quits per 100 employees of the furniture industry. As a further indication of turnover problems, the furniture quit rate for 1968 was almost twice the average for all durable manufacturers. It appears that when the economy is prosperous and jobs are plentiful, furniture employees are quick to seek employment elsewhere. In times of high unemployment, the turnover rate drops considerably, but still remains above the average for all manufacturers.

The level of Negro employment within the furniture industry can be expected to increase during times of full employment. As the national demand for labor increases, many furniture employees, attracted by the higher wages in other industries, are drawn away from the furniture industry. Particularly in the South, where the Negroes are more heavily concentrated, the furniture industry has had to turn, out of economic necessity, to the Negro to replace its work force. Because many of these new employees may have had little previous industrial experience, it can be expected that an unstable work force will continue. An earlier study of the textile industry, which also has a high turnover rate, recommends that management develop "techniques of motivation and worker-job relatedness" [54] designed to cultivate a stable work force.

54. *Ibid.*, p. 31.

TABLE 15

Furniture and All Manufacturing Industries

Labor Turnover by Standard Industrial Classification Groups

1958 and 1968

Per 100 Employees	Year	Total Mfg.	Furniture and Fixtures (SIC 25)	Household Furniture (SIC 251)	Wood Household Furniture (SIC 2511)	Upholstered Household Furniture (SIC 2512)	Mattresses and Bedsprings (SIC 2515)	Office Furniture (SIC 252)
Accessions	1958	3.6	3.8	3.7	4.0	3.1	3.2	2.4
	1968	4.6	6.3	6.5	6.6	5.3	6.4	4.7
New Hires	1958	1.7	2.2	2.1	2.2	2.2	1.6	1.1
	1968	3.5	5.6	5.7	5.8	4.9	5.9	4.2
Separations	1958	4.1	4.2	4.1	4.2	3.4	3.6	2.5
	1968	4.6	6.0	6.1	6.3	4.7	6.3	4.6
Quits	1958	1.1	1.3	1.4	1.5	1.4	0.9	0.7
	1968	2.5	4.1	4.4	4.6	3.5	4.5	2.9
Layoffs	1958	2.6	2.4	2.2	2.2	1.5	2.3	1.5
	1968	1.2	0.8	0.6	0.6	0.4	0.5	0.6

Source: U.S. Bureau of Labor Statistics, Employment and Earnings, United States, 1909-1970, Bulletin No. 1312-7, pp. 33-34, and pp. 61-70.

Unionization

As furniture making began to emerge as an industry, efforts to organize the work force also began to occur, primarily on a local level. In 1873, however, the Furniture Workers Association of North America (FWA) began to organize on a national level. Although it had become affiliated with the American Federation of Labor in 1887, by 1892 another industry union, the Upholsterers International Union of North America (UIU), also affiliated with the AFL, had developed to express the concerns of employees in that industry segment.[55]

In 1896 the FWA merged with the Machine Wood Workers to form the Amalgamated Wood Workers International Union of America (AWW). The newly formed AWW became increasingly involved in jurisdictional disputes with the United Brotherhood of Carpenters and Joiners. In 1902 an AFL executive counsel decision, and later an arbitrator's decision, awarded jurisdiction over all factory woodworkers to the AWW. The Carpenters, however, refused to accept the decision and for ten years fought the AWW. By 1911, what nine years earlier had been the twelfth largest union in the United States (30,000 members), and one of the fastest growing, had been reduced to 4,000 members. On January 10, 1912, the AWW, which could no longer hold out against the much larger Carpenters, was absorbed by them. Thus, the UIU was left as the major union specifically for furniture employees.[56]

By extending its jurisdiction to include a number of allied crafts—mattress making, measuring and hanging of draperies and awnings, fitting slip covers on automobile bodies, and the laying of linoleum and carpets—the UIU was able to triple its membership from 3,500 members in 1914 to 10,700 members in 1929. In this way it attempted to counterbalance losses in one trade with gains in another. When, for example, the mattress- and bedspring-making trade was adversely affected by new machinery and when hotel bed equipment, formerly custom made, began to be mass produced in shops owned by large hotels, the

---

55. Lloyd G. Renolds and Charles C. Killingsworth, *Trade Union Publications* (Baltimore: Johns Hopkins Press, 1944), pp. 119-120, 211, 225 and 313-316.

56. Robert A. Christie, *Empire in Wood* (Ithaca, N.Y.: Cornell University, 1956), pp. 110-119.

union began organizing the rapidly expanding linoleum and craft trades.[57]

In 1937, as a result of the warfare between the AFL and the CIO, a seceding faction of the UIU and the independent organizations affiliated with the CIO organized the United Furniture Workers of America (UFW). The UFW thus became the second furniture-oriented union.[58] From the first days of its existence, the UFW has had Negroes among its membership.[59]

The major membership gains of furniture unions in the late 1930s and early 1940s were confined almost entirely to the North. Unionization is still resisted in various sections of the country, especially notably in the South. A study by the Department of Labor in 1943 revealed that 55 percent of the National Furniture Manufacturers Association's members were unionized, whereas only 10 percent of the southern furniture companies were operating with collective bargaining agreements.[60] A less extensive study in the early 1950s, in which 150 leading southern plants employing 33,395 workers were considered, reported that 31 plants, or approximately 20 percent,[61] had unions. Currently, of the 144 companies belonging to the Southern Manufacturers Association, only 14 are unionized.[62]

In regard to wood household furniture, the major segment of the furniture industry, a Department of Labor study shows that the Pacific states report the highest degree of unionization, and the South and border states report the lowest. In 1970, the Pacific states reported that the ratio of union to nonunion manufacturers was 7 to 10; the South and border states reported 1 to 5 and 1 to 6, respectively. All other regions reported a ratio of 1 to 2, making the overall national ratio 2 to 5.[63]

57. Lewis L. Lorwin, *The American Federation of Labor* (Washington, D.C.: The Brooking Institution, 1933), p. 498.

58. "CIO Carriers War Into Furniture Ranks," *New York Times*, Dec. 10, 1937, p. L 13.

59. United Furniture Workers, *Proceedings of Fifteenth Constitutional Convention*, Memphis, Tennessee, 1968, p. 189.

60. Davis, *op. cit.*, pp. 48-49.

61. *Ibid.*

62. "Workers Vote for Union at La-Z-Boy's South Carolina Plant," *Home Furnishing Daily*, Feb. 25, 1971, p. 7.

63. U.S. Department of Labor, *Industry Wage Survey: Wood Household Furniture Except Upholstered* (Washington: U.S. Government Printing Office, 1970), p. 2.

At present fifteen different unions, ranging from the Teamsters to the Toy Makers and from AFL-CIO affiliates to independents, are found in the furniture industry. Of this number, however, only two are primarily oriented toward the furniture industry: the UFW, with 100 percent of its membership in the furniture industry, and the UIU, with 99 percent. Only one other union reports more than 5 percent of its membership in the industry— the Metal Polishers, Buffers, Platers and Helpers International Union, with 25 percent representation. (In 1969 total membership of the Metal Polishers was only 20,000).[64] Although less than 5 percent of the Carpenters' membership is made up of furniture industry employees, it is the third largest union in the industry and shows signs of being the fastest growing. Currently, between 20,000 and 26,000 furniture workers are members of the Carpenters.[65]

In recent years there have not been significant membership gains in the two major furniture unions. Between 1959 and 1969, UFW membership declined by 25 percent (from 50,000 to 37,500) and the UIU experienced a 6 percent increase (from 56,101 to 60,000). These two unions account for approximately 62 percent of union membership in the furniture industry.[66]

Although the relatively small size of the furniture unions would seem to preclude major industry gains on behalf of Negroes, both the UIU and UFW officially advocated nondiscrimination prior to the enactment of the 1964 Civil Rights Act. As early as 1950, the UFW had developed machinery for creating a Civil Rights Committee, and the UIU constitution has long provided for nondiscrimination.

---

64. U.S. Department of Labor, *Directory of National and International Labor Unions in the United States, 1969* (Washington: U.S. Government Printing Office, 1970), pp. 74 and 98.

65. Personal interview.

66. U.S. Department of Labor, *Directory, 1969, op. cit.,* pp. 26 and 45. Also *Directory, 1959,* pp. 35 and 47.

CHAPTER III

Negro Employment to 1960

Furniture making in America had its beginning sometime shortly after the arrival of the Mayflower in 1620. Because of the Tunnage Act, the Mayflower was required to include among its occupants someone capable of making casks to contain the ship's provisions. Thus, John Alden, a twenty-one-year-old cooper, became the first trained woodworker to reach the New World.[67]

FROM COLONIAL TIMES TO 1840

For the next fifty years an increasing number of European immigrants settled in the colonies, among them "skilled craftsmen . . ., not merely carpenters and housewrights, but turners, joiners, cabinetmakers, and even carvers; and these men were quite capable of making all the furniture in fashion." [68] By 1700 furniture making was an established business in America.[69]

For approximately the next century and a half the structure of the furniture industry changed very little. It continued to be characterized by individual craftsmen producing custom-made furniture. Almost without exception these craftsmen were of European descent. Except for a few free Negro cabinetmakers, Negroes found in the furniture industry were slaves who were either owned by a cabinetmaker or made to perform such work in the service of a plantation. It was not until the twentieth century that Negroes became an important element in the furniture work force.

The Cabinetmaker

Initially, quality pieces of furniture were imported from abroad, and only the rougher kinds of furniture were made in this country. By 1700, however, skilled artisans, many trained

---

67. Ormsbee, *op cit.*, pp. 22-23.

68. Esther Singleton, *The Furniture of Our Forefathers*, Vol. III (New York: Doubleday, Page and Co., 1900), p. 173.

69. Ormsbee, *op cit.*, p. 37.

in the cabinetmaking shops of Europe, had opened shops of their own. Except for an occasional very successful shop, which could employ an apprentice or two, these were generally one-man operations.

During the first half of the eighteenth century a few Negroes were to be found in the emerging furniture industry.

The number of . . . cabinetmakers in all the colonies increased as various regions of the country became prosperous. . . . Cabinetmakers everywhere, however, were loosely organized, dependent upon the apprenticeship system for the training of new workers. There were guilds in many towns or counties; there were itinerate joiners working their way from town to town; and in the south slaves trained in carpentry and cabinetmaking carried on their craft on many of the big plantations, some, indeed, working in the shops of cabinetmakers.[70]

Although furniture was made in all the colonies, it was in New England and the Middle Atlantic states, areas with few Negroe residents, that the first concentration of the industry occurred. As the southern colonies became increasingly agricultural, cabinetmaking declined in importance. In Philadelphia and points north, however, furniture became increasingly important. Connecticut, Massachusetts, Rhode Island, Pennsylvania, and New York became major centers of furniture production. In addition to being population centers, these states also had seaports which gave manufacturers access to imported woods [71] and provided a means of transporting products to distant markets.

As the demand for furniture increased and as more craftsmen entered the furniture industry, product and job specialization began to occur. A gradual increase in the size of many cabinetmaking shops resulted, as more than one phase of workmanship was often combined into one shop.[72] By the early 1800s this gradual change in the industry's structure could be dramatically seen in shops like that of Duncan Phyfe of New York, in which over 100 journeymen, including cabinetmakers, carvers, turners, and upholsterers, were employed.[73]

---

70. Ethel Hall Bjerkoe, *The Cabinetmakers of America* (Garden City, N.Y.: Doubleday and Co., 1957), p. 10.

71. Victor S. Clark, *History of Manufacturing in the United States*, Vol. I (New York: McGraw-Hill Book Co., 1929), p. 472.

72. Bjerkoe, *op. cit.*, p. 10.

73. Oliver, *op. cit.*, p. 52.

As the shops of cabinetmakers gradually grew larger it became possible for a few Negroes to find employment in them. Because of the heavy industry concentration outside the South and the abundance of skilled European immigrants, however, the Negro continued to be a negligible part of the furniture industry.

The Slave as Cabinetmaker

Since cabinetmaking in the United States was a craft almost exclusively monopolized by people of European descent, the Negro became a part of the craft only when it became economically advantageous for him to be utilized. Only in the southern states were any sizable number of Negroes trained in the furniture-making crafts; those trained were almost always slaves.

Prior to the Revolutionary War it was considered cheaper to purchase the indentures of immigrant cabinetmakers than to train a slave. However, with the commencement of the war, one source of cheap skilled labor was eliminated, and another source had to be found: the increased training of slaves.[74]

Since it was not necessary to train all slaves as artisans and mechanics, only the most intelligent slaves were selected and trained for such work as carpentry and cabinetmaking.[75] An example of such a use of slaves is to be found in the furniture of Thomas Jefferson's home. "After his presidency . . . such new pieces of furniture as were needed at Monticello were made on the place. John Hemings, the slave who became a skillful cabinetmaker, and James Dinsmore, one of Jefferson's master builders, constructed most of the pieces."[76]

The cabinetmaking that was performed on the southern plantations was often done by a highly skilled slave carpenter rather than a master cabinetmaker. "Such a trade as that of a slave carpenter comprehended a great many operations. Often such an artisan performed the duties of a wheelwright, sawyer, cabinetmaker, clapboard maker, cooper, and, in fact, the making of practically anything made of wood."[77]

---

74. Raymond B. Pinchbeck, *The Virginia Negro Artisan and Tradesman* (Richmond, Va.: The William Byrd Press, Inc., 1926), pp. 32-33.

75. W. D. Weatherford, *The Negro from Africa to America* (New York: George H. Doran Co., 1924), p. 222.

76. Marie G. Kimball, *The Furnishings of Monticello* (Charlottesville, Va.: The Thomas Jefferson Memorial Foundation, 1946), p. 8.

77. Pinchbeck, *op. cit.*, pp. 32-33.

Not all Negroes trained in the craft of cabinetmaking were found on the plantations of the South. There were some who worked in the shops of southern cabinetmakers. In Charleston, South Carolina, for example,

Elfe (Thomas) and his partner Fisher (John), with their employees, including some Negro slave craftsmen, made bedsteads of poplar and mahogany, desks, picture frames and brick moulds of mahogany, straight chairs, easy chairs, French chairs, sofas and couches, card tables, tea tables, side tables, breakfast tables, dining tables, chests of drawers, Venetian blinds, fire screens, and numerous other articles of occasional furniture.[78]

Later, after the dissolution of his partnership with Thomas Elfe, John Fisher advertised in 1771 that he "had purchased of Mr. Stephen Townsend his Stock-in-Trade and Negroes brought up in the business, which he now carries on at the House in Meeting Street where Mr. Townsend formerly lived." [79]

It was not unusual for capable slave cabinetmakers to be passed from father to son along with other valuable business property. The junior Thomas Elfe (1759-1825) carried on his father's business after inheriting not only his working tools and benches but also his "Father's three Negroes." [80]

Although most Negroes in the furniture-making crafts were slaves either on the plantations or in shops of cabinetmakers of the South, there were a few free Negro cabinetmakers to be found as well as white cabinetmakers advertising for Negro employees.[81] Again, these free Negro cabinetmakers were found predominantly in the South, for it was in the South that "the Negro developed highest in occupations. This was possible for the reason that in the antebellum South the Negro, constituting more than one-third of the total population, furnished the chief labor supply of that section." [82] In some southern states it has been estimated that for every white craftsmen that could be found, there were at least two Negro craftsmen of most kinds.[83]

---

78. Oliver, *op. cit.*, p. 18.

79. *Ibid.*, p. 46.

80. *Ibid.*, p. 18.

81. *Ibid.*, p. 53.

82. Lorenzo J. Greene and Carter G. Woodson, *The Negro Wage Earner* (New York: Van Rees Press, 1930), p. 7.

83. Charles H. Wesley, *Negro Labor in the United States* (New York: Vanguard Press, Inc., 1927), p. 142.

The Negro working in the furniture crafts prior to the Civil War was not solely limited to the South. Such cities as St. Louis, Philadelphia, and Cincinnati, and the state of Massachusetts reported Negroes employed in furniture making. By 1859 Philadelphia reported the employment of twenty Negro cabinetmakers, one Negro chairmaker, and four Negro upholsterers. One year later Cincinnati recorded the employment of three Negro cabinetmakers and Massachusetts recorded one Negro cabinetmaker, two Negro chairmakers, and nine Negro upholsterers. Southern cities such as New Orleans and Charleston, however, remained among the leaders in employing Negroes. In 1850, New Orleans reported two Negroes and seventeen mulattoes working as upholsterers. For the same year Charleston employed four Negro cabinetmakers, three Negro tinners, and two Negro upholsterers.[84]

THE EMERGENCE OF THE FURNITURE FACTORY

During the early years of the nineteenth century furniture making in the United States began to shift gradually from individual craftsmen using hand tools in small shops to a factory system with greater emphasis on machine production. Such a shift would ultimately prove beneficial to the Negro, but it was to be more than a hundred years before major employment gains would occur.

Most of the early furniture factories were located in the East near rivers where water power could be easily harnessed to machinery. The use of such machinery not only shifted the industry from a shop to a factory basis but also increased product and job specialization. Power mechanisms made this development economical from an administrative standpoint and the enlarged market that came with a growing population made it commercially possible.[85] By lowering production costs, water power helped to increase furniture consumption.

By the middle of the century water power was supplanted by the steam engine. No longer was the size or location of a factory limited by the availability of water. In addition, specialization continued as power was now more easily distributed

---

84. *Ibid.*, pp. 35-48.

85. Clark, *op. cit.*, pp. 472-473.

to smaller units of machinery.[86] The result was a gradual change in the necessary skill level of the work force. Now, rather than being heavily dependent on the highly skilled craftsmen so important in earlier years, more and more reliance was being placed on semiskilled factory hands. This category of work would ultimately provide a major source of employment for the Negro in the furniture industry.

Westward Movement of the Industry

Although the furniture industry continued to be heavily concentrated in the East, with the states of New York, Pennsylvania, and Massachusetts dominating the industry, as the population of the country moved west and as the need for new timber resources increased, the furniture industry also began moving west. During the period immediately preceding the Civil War, Ohio became the fourth largest furniture-producing state, and Cincinnati became the principal furniture-making center of the West. With the abundance of hardwoods and the development of large steam plants employing 100 or more workers, production costs became low enough for Cincinnati's goods to compete in markets throughout the South and West. As a result, the output of these factories increased for a series of years at the rate of 25 percent a year.[87] For the Negro, however, this was to be of little consequence, as very few Negroes lived in or around these western furniture centers.

By 1850 the total number of men engaged in furniture making and allied trades was reported at 83,580. Of this number, 37,359 were cabinet and chair makers. An additional 12,672 workers were listed as joiners who may have been working at either carpentry or furniture making.[88] Although no statistics are available as to how many of these workers were Negroes, it would seem likely, based on later figures, that the level was at 1 percent or less.

The Civil War brought economic stagnation to the furniture industry.[89] Shortly after the war, however, as the demand for new furniture increased,[90] the westward expansion of the industry

86. A. P. Johnson and Marta K. Sironen, *Manual of the Furniture Arts and Crafts* (Grand Rapids, Mich.: A. P. Johnson Co., 1928), p. 378.
87. Clark, *op. cit.*, p. 474.
88. Ormsbee, *op. cit.*, p. 89.
89. Johnson, *op. cit.*, p. 80.
90. *Ibid.*, p. 247.

continued with renewed emphasis. In the Central Atlantic and Great Lakes states there were many factories going into operation, whereas there had been very few when the war began.

By 1870 furniture factories were widely distributed. The distribution, however, continued to be in areas of relatively low Negro concentration. Centers of furniture production had arisen in Cincinnati and St. Louis, although important factories were beginning to develop in Jamestown, New York; Grand Rapids, Michigan; Chicago, Illinois; Indianapolis, Indiana; and the hardwood regions of Tennessee. Only in the hardwood regions of Tennessee and the cities of St. Louis and Indianapolis did the level of Negro population exceed 2.8 percent. In these three areas the Negro population ranged from approximately 6 percent to 10 percent of total population.[91] Nevertheless, New York, Massachusetts, and Pennsylvania remained the three highest-ranking states in total employment in the industry, with Boston, New York City, and Philadelphia continuing to make a large share of the high-grade furniture produced in this country.[92]

As an indication of the lack of employment opportunities for Negroes in the furniture industry, the Bureau of the Census reported that as late as 1900 none of the leading furniture states had a population which was even 3 percent Negro. New York, Massachusetts, and Pennsylvania reported only 1.4, 1.1, and 2.5 percent of their respective populations as Negro. Consequently, New York reported only ten Negro "furniture manufactory employees" and eleven Negro cabinetmakers; Massachusetts, seven "employees" and three cabinetmakers; and Pennsylvania twelve "employees" and nine cabinetmakers. The opportunities for Negroes were little better in the emerging centers. In Michigan, Illinois, Indiana, Ohio, and Missouri, Negroes made up only 0.7, 1.8, 2.3, 2.3 and 5.2 percent of their respective populations. As would be expected, these states also reported low employment levels for Negroes. Michigan employed three "furniture manufactory employees" and four cabinetmakers; Illinois, four and seven; Indiana, two and four; Ohio, eleven and zero; and Missouri, seven and five.[93]

---

91. U.S. Department of the Interior, Census Office, *The Tenth Census: 1880*, Tables 23 and 24.

92. Clark, *op. cit.*, pp. 128, 147-148, and 185.

93. U.S. Bureau of the Census, *U.S. Census of Population, 1900: Negroes in the United States*, Tables 26 and 55.

By the late 1800s Cincinnati had become the leading furniture city in America.[94] That position, however, was not retained for long. As the timber resources around Cincinnati began to diminish, the industry concentration shifted northward to Grand Rapids, in the forests of Michigan.[95] By the turn of the century Grand Rapids had achieved the distinction of being the "Furniture City of the United States." [96]

Michigan forests, being no more inexhaustible than those of Ohio, were soon seriously depleted and Grand Rapids began to lose this primary advantage over other areas. Although in 1920 Michigan ranked second only to New York in the value of furniture produced, a new challenger was rising in the South that would eventually outrun all others.[97]

Industry Movement to the South

There is little doubt that one of the greatest factors contributing to the current level of Negro employment in the furniture industry is the concentration of the industry in the South. As of 1860, 92.2 percent of the entire Negro population in the United States was located in the South.[98] Consequently, until the furniture industry began to emerge in the South, the Negro had relatively little opportunity to be a part of it. Until the middle of the twentieth century, the Negro's advancement in the furniture industry was almost exclusively tied to the advancement of the southern furniture industry.

Under the plantation system, the South had been comparatively indifferent to manufacturing. Thus, the South had to depend upon both imports and trained slaves to supply items such as furniture.

The whole tendency of the economic system in the old South was to cultivate individuality and to encourage independent action among the planters. It followed, then, that the overwhelming majority of the Southern people preferred to devote themselves to a pursuit that each one could carry on independently without any of those combinations of men

---

94. Oliver, *op. cit.*, pp. 88-89.

95. *Ibid.*, pp. 89-91.

96. David N. Thomas, "A History of Southern Furniture," *Furniture World*, October 12, 1967, p. 25.

97. Oliver, *op. cit.*, pp. 91-92.

98. Greene, *op. cit.*, p. 7.

or capital which would have been necessary had they engaged in manu-factures.[99]

With the abolition of slavery, the indifference to manufactur-ing began to change and by the 1880s furniture manufacturing, along with other industries, began emerging in the South. As northern investors established textile plants in the Carolina Piedmont and steelmaking developed in Alabama, furniture fac-tories built by small-town business and professional men began turning out inexpensive lines of furniture for local markets in the Southeast. Most of these plants appeared in Virginia, Georgia, and Tennessee.[100]

Furniture manufacturing in the South differed from almost all other American furniture sectors. Whereas most furniture manu-facturing centers of the nineteenth century had been started by European cabinetmakers, in the South the men were American born. They came from plantations or farms and few were ex-perienced in the art of carpentry or cabinetmaking. Although some manufacturers from the Northeast came south to take ad-vantage of the available hardwood forests and the abundance of inexpensive labor, the early industry was primarily the result of local investment.[101]

The early years of the southern furniture plants were quite profitable, as the inexpensive products found a ready market among low-income southerners. With the success of these early plants, more and more entrepreneurs were drawn into the furniture industry—particularly in North Carolina and Virginia. In High Point, North Carolina, for example, there were over a dozen plants operating at the turn of the century. Every few months a new furniture factory went into operation, as virtually every business and professional man in town invested in the new industry.[102] Not only High Point, but also other relatively small North Carolina and Virginia cities such as Hickory, Lenoir, Drexel, Thomasville, Bassett, Altavista, and Martinsville were locations for prominent furniture factories.[103] By 1910 the south-

---

99. C. F. Korstain, *The Economic Development of the Furniture Industry of the South and Its Future Dependence upon Forestry,* Economic Paper No. 57 (Raleigh: North Carolina Department of Conservation and Development, 1926), p. 9.

100. Thomas, *op. cit.,* pp. 13-14.

101. *Ibid.,* pp. 9 and 14.

102. *Ibid.,* pp. 14 and 25.

103. Oliver, *op. cit.,* pp. 92-93, and interviews.

ern industry was attracting serious attention from the trade's national observers.[104]

In the early years of the southern furniture industry, employment was often almost exclusively restricted to white men.[105] In 1900 North Carolina reported only 23 Negro "furniture manufactory employees" and 13 Negro cabinetmakers, while Virginia reported 22 and 27, respectively. Although in Tennessee and Georgia the industry concentration was not as great as that in North Carolina and Virginia, the Negroes in these states were nevertheless more likely to find employment in the furniture industry. For the same year, Tennessee reported 52 "furniture manufactory employees" and 30 cabinetmakers and Georgia reported 174 and 54.

The statistics for these four states are not large in comparison to total industry employment, but they nevertheless represented approximately 60 percent of total Negro "furniture manufactory employees" and 37 percent of total Negro cabinetmakers in the United States.[106] In addition, these states held a potential for an increasing level of Negro employment, as the populations in North Carolina, Virginia, Tennessee, and Georgia in 1900 were 33.0, 35.6, 23.8, and 46.7 percent black, respectively.[107]

In interviews with southern industry representatives it was not unusual to find that a few Negroes were employed in some of their original work forces. These Negroes, however, usually represented a very small minority and were generally employed in the more menial jobs. On the other hand, there were examples of some southern furniture plants that employed large percentages of Negroes.

In the saw and planing mills the Negroes and whites usually worked together. Thus, in a North Carolina lumber mill in 1903, out of 150 employees 135 were Negroes; a larger mill in Arkansas in the same year employed 150 persons, 75 of whom were Negroes; in Louisiana another mill employed 250 Negroes out of 500 employees; in a stave factory in South Carolina all of the 129 workers except four were Negroes. In some woodworking factories Negro laborers were employed

---

104. Thomas, *op. cit.*, pp. 25 and 33.

105. M. Eleanor Craig, "Recent History of the North Carolina Furniture Manufacturing Industry with Special Attention to Locational Factors," (unpublished Ph.D. dissertation, Duke University, 1959), p. 140.

106. Of a total of 456 Negro "furniture manufactory employees" and 340 Negro cabinetmakers in the United States as of 1900, none were women.

107. U.S. Bureau of the Census, *U.S. Census of Population, 1900: Negroes in the United States*, Tables 26 and 55.

exclusively. According to an investigator of the Negroes in the Black Belt in 1899, two large chair factories in Marietta, Georgia, employed practically none but Negro workmen. The work was light and much of it was done in the homes.[108]

It was frequently argued that Negroes were generally an unreliable source of labor in that they were not as responsible as white workers.[109] Although in certain situations there may have been some basis for such an attitude, it was not unknown for some woodworking plants to hire Negroes in preference to whites. Frequently, in some of the smaller woodworking plants, such as barrel or stave factories, some managers indicated that they found the Negro to be quite reliable—in fact, more reliable than the whites. "According to an investigator, a barrel manufacturer at Jonesboro, Alabama, said he employed Negroes because he found it difficult to get white men who would work steadily." [110]

An additional factor that often barred Negroes from employment opportunities in the southern furniture industry was the race consciousness of whites.[111] The development of the plantation system had been detrimental not only to Negroes but also to many whites, as large numbers of whites were dispossessed and denied any real participation in the life of the South. White people often developed bitterness toward the Negro slave, who appeared to be employed and living under more favorable conditions on plantations than were those whites who were generally excluded from the system. Thus, the establishment of industry in the South often provided whites with a chance to reenter society.[112] Consequently, some whites were reluctant to let Negroes share in employment opportunities when there was an ample supply of white labor.

Race consciousness as a bar to Negro employment is illustrated by the following example from a southern stave factory in 1899.

When asked by an investigator why he hired no Negro help the employer expressed the general feeling when he replied, "People don't think it right to employ Negro labor when there is white to be had." "This," continued the investigator, "was the universal feeling among

108. Greene, *op. cit.*, pp. 125-126.

109. Rowan, *op. cit.*, pp. 49-52.

110. Greene, *op. cit.*, p. 126.

111. *Ibid.*, p. 127.

112. Rowan, *op. cit.*, pp. 45-46.

those who did not hold that the hiring of labor was purely a matter of cents and not sentiment. So strong was this feeling among the farmers that when a manufacturer named Adams opened a stave factory in competition with Molocks and attempted to run it with Negro labor the farmers would not sell him lumber. Molock's factory, I am told, was just lined with bolts but Adams couldn't buy any at all unless he shipped them on the railroad, and that was too expensive. Nobody would sell and he just had to give up. He didn't hire any white labor, but he sold out to a man who has never hired anything else." Commenting upon the novel procedure, the investigator said, "Boycotts, where the boycotters refuse to buy have been common enough ever since the Revolutionary fathers set the example. But a boycott where Anglo-Saxon men refuse to sell is novel in our annals. No mixed motives of sentiment and economy could be counted on to keep it alive. It was pure self-sacrifice in behalf of a cause." [113]

When Negroes could find employment they were often denied access to the more skilled jobs by the prevalent opinion that they were incompetent to perform such tasks.

Said a large employer of Negro labor in 1891, "The Negro is the best common laborer, but he cannot acquire the skill of the white man—at lease he don't." According to another, "When muscle alone is wanted, we find good Negro labor very efficient, but when some degree of judgement is to be exercised, we prefer white labor." [114]

These opinions cannot be applied generally to the southern furniture industry, for in some plants much of the work, whether unskilled or skilled, was performed by Negroes.

In . . . mills such as woodworking, furniture, wagon and carriage factories Negroes were performing semiskilled and skilled labor. Among these artisans were sawyers, trimmers, turners, cabinetmakers, edgers, block setters, ax men, planers, cutters, finishers, and others. This fact is attested by the employers themselves. A mill owner of North Carolina reported in 1902 that "out of 135 Negroes 50 were performing skilled labor as firemen, saw setters, edgemen, trimmers, girders, train men and sawyers." They were considered as skillful as the whites. In Arkansas 50 out of 75 Negroes were running machines and serving in other skilled capacities. They were earning from $1.25 to $4.00 a day. In Virginia a large wood working concern reported 235 Negro hands, of whom 175 were semiskilled workers.[115]

In the early days of furniture manufacturing in the South, black employment varied considerably from community to community and did not follow a regional pattern. In a 1920 survey

---

113. Greene, *op. cit.*, pp. 127-128.

114. *Ibid.*, p. 127.

115. *Ibid.*, p. 126.

of the furniture industry in North Carolina, Virginia, and Tennessee, it was found that unlike the textile industry, furniture manufacturing was not solely a white man's industry. In various cities of the three states there were numerous Negro workers, although in other cities no Negro labor was to be found in furniture factories. In the industry as a whole, however, whites continued to greatly outnumber Negroes. Yet, in spite of this apparent hiring discrimination, there were no noticeable differences in the wages of whites and blacks in the plants where the two were employed. This study also reported that few female workers were to be found in the plants of any of the states studied. Those women who were employed were usually found in the finishing department, where both white and black women worked together.[116]

The shift of much furniture manufacturing from the North to the South was accomplished primarily by southerners entering the industry rather than by northerners migrating. By taking advantage of the timber resources, the abundance of low-cost labor, and the developing southern market, these men were able to lay the foundation for what would ultimately become a major southern industry. As a result of the abundance of available labor, furniture manufacturers could often be quite selective as to whom they would employ. When this abundance of labor was combined with white race consciousness and prejudicial opinions concerning the Negro's character and abilities, an environment was created in which Negroes were often excluded from employment opportunities. Not only Negroes but also women were often excluded from employment consideration; thus, whereas labor in textile plants was primarily white and female, furniture labor was primarily white and male.[117] This early employment pattern tended to retard the growth of Negro employment in the furniture industry for the next several decades.

FROM 1900 TO THE DEPRESSION

By 1900 Negroes made up approximately 2 percent of "furniture manufactory employees" (Table 16). As Table 17 indicates,

---

116. Abraham Berglund, George T. Starnes, and Frank T. de Vyver, *Labor in the Industrial South* (Richmond, Va.: The Institute for Research in the Social Sciences, University of Virginia, 1930), p. 21.

117. Rowan, *op. cit.*, p. 56.

TABLE 16. *Furniture Industry*
Total Employment by Race and Sex
United States, 1900–1960

	All Employees			Male			Female		
	Total	Negro	Percent Negro	Total	Negro	Percent Negro	Total	Negro	Percent Negro
1900 [a]	23,078	456	2.0	21,842	456	2.1	1,236	—	—
1910 [b]	160,271	4,254	2.7	152,382	4,090	2.7	7,889	164	2.1
1920 [b, c]	90,989	4,164	4.6	81,506	3,520	4.3	9,483	644	6.8
1930 [b]	268,098	7,934	3.0	246,610	7,324	3.0	21,488	610	2.8
1940	225,675	8,123	3.6	204,411	7,518	3.7	21,264	605	2.8
1950	330,243	20,116	6.1	278,874	16,748	6.2	51,369	3,368	6.6
1960	376,694	27,938	7.4	311,556	23,569	7.6	65,138	4,279	6.6

Source: *U.S. Census of Population*

1900: *Special Reports, Occupations,* Table 1 and *Negroes in the United States,* Table 26.
1910: Volume IV, *Occupation Statistics,* Table VI.
1920: Volume IV, *Occupations,* Table 5.
1930: Volume V, *General Report on Occupations,* Table 2.
1940: Volume III, *The Labor Force,* Part I, Table 76.
1950: Volume II, *Characteristics of the Population,* Part I, Table 133.
1960: *U.S. Summary,* PC(1)1D, Table 213.

[a] Furniture manufactory employees.
[b] Furniture factories.
[c] Laborers and operatives only.

TABLE 17. *Furniture Industry*
Regional Location of Negro Furniture
Manufactory Employees and Cabinetmakers, 1900

	Furniture Manufactory Employees		Cabinetmakers	
	Total Negroes	Percent of U.S. Total	Total Negroes	Percent of U.S. Total
New England	13	2.8	5	1.5
Southern North Atlantic	30	6.6	22	6.4
North Atlantic Division	43	9.4	27	7.9
Northern South Atlantic	35	7.7	51	15.0
Southern South Atlantic	205	45.0	107	31.5
South Atlantic Division	240	52.7	158	46.5
Eastern North Central	20	4.4	17	5.0
Western North Central	15	3.3	9	2.7
North Central Division	35	7.7	26	7.7
Eastern South Central	101	22.1	68	20.0
Western South Central	35	7.7	61	17.9
South Central Division	136	29.8	129	37.9
Rocky Mountain	—	—	—	—
Basin & Plateau	—	—	—	—
Pacific	2	0.4	—	—
Western Division	2	0.4	—	—
United States	456	100.0	340	100.0

Source: *U.S. Census of Population, 1900: Negroes in the United States,*
Table 26.

the South employed 82.5 percent of all Negroes in the industry.
North Carolina, South Carolina, Georgia, and Florida alone
accounted for 45.0 percent of total Negro employment, with
Georgia being by far the major employer and North Carolina
ranking a distant second. Among Negro cabinetmakers, 84.4
percent were employed in the South. The same four states were
leaders in terms of Negro employment, employing 31.5 percent
of the national total, with Georgia again being the major employer.

At the turn of the century the relatively few furniture factories that employed Negroes generally restricted them to unskilled jobs. It continued to be a widely held belief that "in the heavy work of these (furniture) plants, Negroes were . . . superior to other laborers, but they were not [superior] in the skilled factory work." [118] Although they could become good masons, carpenters, blacksmiths, firemen, and engineers, it continued to be believed that the number of Negroes who could do fine cabinetwork was small. Thus, the common prejudicial opinions discussed earlier continued to hinder the Negro's advancement in the furniture industry.

By 1910 the level of Negro employment had increased slightly to 2.7 percent. Although Negroes continued to be heavily concentrated in relatively unskilled jobs, Table 18 indicates that a few were beginning to be found in the more skilled categories as well as in white collar positions.

With the outbreak of war in Europe, the resulting disruption in trade was particularly damaging to the southern furniture industry. Because of the loss of the South's overseas cotton market, furniture sales in the South sharply declined, and southern producers began to give more attention to national marketing. Success in the northern market, combined with government orders for furniture, stimulated further expansion of southern furniture manufacturing and the establishment of a marketing center.[119]

An additional consequence of the war and the attendant scarcity of male labor was that furniture plants, out of necessity, turned to women as a source of employees. As of 1920, women represented approximately 10 percent of the furniture work force, whereas only ten years earlier they had been less than 5 percent. During the same time Negro women were used to a greater degree than before, but their numbers did not exceed 3.4 percent of the total work force. In a government survey of four furniture plants in 1918, it was found that although some Negro women were operating various pieces of equipment, the majority were found in such unskilled jobs as furniture polishing.[120]

---

118. Wesley, *op. cit.*, p. 246.

119. Thomas, *op. cit.*, pp. 47 and 50.

120. U.S. Department of Labor, *The Negro at Work during the World War and during Reconstruction* (Washington: U.S. Government Printing Office, 1921), p. 125.

TABLE 18. *Furniture Industry*
Major Job Categories by Race and Sex
United States, 1910

	All Employees			Male			Female		
	Total	Negro	Percent Negro	Total	Negro	Percent Negro	Total	Negro	Percent Negro
Supervisors[a]	10,082	61	0.6	9,895	60	0.6	187	1	0.5
Office and clerical[b]	4,700	29	0.6	3,276	26	0.8	1,424	3	0.2
Cabinetmakers	32,280	270	0.8	32,272	269	0.8	8	1	12.5
Caners and seaters	2,610	370	14.2	1,712	279	16.3	898	91	10.1
Laborers	23,571	1,376	5.8	23,055	1,365	5.9	516	11	2.1
Repairers	1,070	176	16.4	1,036	171	16.5	34	5	14.7
Teamsters	2,019	183	9.1	2,019	183	9.1	—	—	—
Upholsterers	17,555	797	4.5	16,487	772	4.7	1,068	25	2.3
Painters	5,485	91	1.7	5,337	90	1.7	148	1	0.7
Finishers	8,270	87	1.1	8,169	86	1.1	101	1	1.0
Packers and wrappers	2,820	101	3.6	2,566	99	3.9	254	2	0.8
Others	49,809	713	1.4	46,558	690	1.5	3,251	23	0.7
Total	160,271	4,254	2.7	152,382	4,090	2.7	7,889	164	2.1

Source: U.S. Bureau of the Census, *Negro Population: 1790-1915*, Table 22.

[a] Includes "Manufacturers and Proprietors," "Officials," Managers and Superintendents," and "Foremen and Overseers."

[b] Includes "Clerk (general)," "Clerk (shipping)," "Messenger, Errand and Office Boys," and "Stenographers and Typewriters."

Shortly prior to World War I, electrical power had been found to have applications in woodworking plants, but its real impact was not to be felt until after the war.[121] As more and more manufacturers began switching from steam power to electricity so as to avail themselves of high-speed individual electric machinery, the industry was able to take full advantage of the war-created, suppressed demands of consumers. The market for medium- and low-priced home furnishings, the area of southern emphasis, was unusually good.[122] As a result of continued southern expansion, particularly in North Carolina, national recognition of southern furniture production was solidly established during the 1920s. In addition, by 1929 North Carolina had become the fifth-ranking state behind New York, Illinois, Indiana, and Michigan in overall furniture production and first place in the output of bedroom and dining room furniture.[123]

As Table 19 shows, from 1919 to 1929 all regions showed an increase in the number of furniture jobs. Only the southern and Pacific states, however, showed an increase in the percentage of total national employment. Thus, the industry was beginning a slow-but-steady movement to the West Coast, particularly to California, where both lumber and a market were available. More important for the Negro, however, was the continued industry concentration in the South. Whereas certain industries of the South continued to be all-white, furniture manufacturing had begun employing blacks.[124] In fact, by 1930 the level of Negro employment in the total industry had risen to 3.0 percent. Nevertheless, Negroes continued to be primarily restricted to working as common laborers.[125]

THE DEPRESSION

Although the Great Depression severely affected the furniture industry, it nevertheless, in a backhanded way, contributed to what was then considered a sizable increase in the relative standing of Negroes in the industry.

---

121. Johnson, *op. cit.*, p. 382.

122. Thomas, *op. cit.*, p. 50.

123. *Ibid.*, p. 66.

124. Robert C. Weaver, *Negro Labor: A National Problem,* (New York: Harcourt, Brace and Co., 1946), p. 8.

125. Maurice R. Davie, *Negroes in American Society* (New York: McGraw Hill Book Co., 1949), p. 88.

TABLE 19. *Furniture Industry*
Regional Distribution of Employment, 1919 and 1929

	United States	New England	Middle Atlantic	East North Central	West North Central	South Atlantic	East South Central	West South Central	Mountain	Pacific
Employment—1929	193,399	12,246	39,947	82,829	7,652	27,681	6,972	4,122	292	11,658
Employment—1919	144,423	9,031	35,575	67,741	6,840	13,104	5,081	2,137	246	4,668
Increase from 1919 to 1929	48,976	3,215	4,372	15,088	812	14,577	1,891	1,985	46	6,990
Percent of U.S. Total —1929	100.0	6.3	20.7	42.8	4.0	14.3	3.6	2.1	0.2	6.0
Percent of U.S. Total —1919	100.0	6.3	24.6	46.9	4.7	9.1	3.5	1.5	0.2	3.2

Source: U.S. Bureau of the Census, *Location of Manufactures: 1899-1929*, p. 18.

From 1929 to 1933 the output of America's furniture producers dropped from $659 million to $235 million and the number of producers declined from 3,000 to 2,000.[126] As would be expected, the economic conditions that eliminated a third of the entire industry also drastically affected industry employment and wages. A Department of Commerce study of the household furniture industry, using 1939 as a base year, showed that the employment index dropped from 111.9 in 1929 to 57.4 in 1932 and that the wage index dropped even more severely, from 154.9 to 47.0. Not until after 1940 did the industry recover the ground it had lost.[127]

Although the furniture industry in all regions suffered greatly from the depression, the South suffered the least, and ultimately profited from the reduced competition.

Because of their emphasis on medium and low cost merchandise, Southern producers had a larger market than their Northern competitors. While some Southern manufacturers either went into bankruptcy or curtailed their operations, most of them were able to stay in business even at lower levels of profits. Northern competitors could not adjust so easily, due to higher labor costs and to smaller markets for high priced merchandise.[128]

Thus, as many nonsouthern employees, almost all white, were being forced out of the industry, many southern employees, including Negroes, were able to retain their jobs. The result was that the southern industry, as well as Negroes, were able to increase their relative position within the industry.

This southern advancement is further illustrated by the fact that between 1928 and 1936 the percentage of American furniture shipments which originated on railroads in the South rose from 36.8 percent to 43.1 percent. By 1937, North Carolina and Virginia accounted for 38 percent of all bedroom furniture and 37 percent of all dining room furniture produced in the United States. In addition, during the depression years North Carolina moved ahead of Michigan, Indiana, and Illinois in terms of overall furniture production, to rank second behind New York. It is clear that although the furniture industry of the South shared with all America the damaging effects of the

126. Thomas, *op. cit.*, pp. 67-69.

127. Edward R. Killam, *Household Furniture: A Statistical Handbook*, Industrial Series No. 8 (Washington: U.S. Department of Commerce, June 1944), p. 14.

128. Thomas, *op. cit.*, p. 72.

Great Depression, that event was a factor in the coming of southern domination of American furniture production.[129]

An indication of the Negro's advancement is seen in Table 16. Although, as noted earlier, the decade of the 1930s was a period of declining employment in the furniture industry, Negroes, by virtue of their being heavily concentrated in the South, were somewhat protected from job losses. Between 1930 and 1940 total furniture employment dropped by approximately 16 percent, or 42,423, with almost all of the decline being experienced by white men. The level of Negro men employed actually rose by approximately 2.6 percent to a new high of 7,518. The level of Negro women employed remained quite stable, as it declined by only 5 to 605, or a level of 0.8 percent, while total female employment declined by 224, or 1.0 percent. All in all, Negroes as a percent of total furniture employment rose from 3.0 percent to 3.6 percent during the depression decade.

In addition to not adversely affecting the level of Negro employment, as might have been expected, the 1930s also saw Negroes being employed to a greater extent in semiskilled jobs. For example, Negroes in North Carolina, in addition to comprising one-sixth of the laborer category, now accounted for one-thirteenth of all operative jobs in the state. In general, with the close of the depression decade, Negroes were gradually increasing their overall level of participation in the furniture industry, most finding employment as unskilled laborers in lumberyards and veneer and shipping departments. Nevertheless, there appeared to be a slight opening up of opportunities for Negroes as machine operators.[130]

FROM WORLD WAR II TO 1960

American involvement in World War II provided the final step necessary for the South's emergence as the dominant furniture-producing region in the country. In conjunction with this development, the Negro achieved a major breakthrough in terms of employment opportunities in the furniture industry. Although the largest gains in black employment were in the South, all regions of the United States participated in the increased opportunities for Negroes.

---

129. *Ibid.*

130. Craig, *op. cit.*, pp. 140-141.

The initial impact of the war was to virtually eliminate the production of civilian furniture because of the shortage of labor available for nonessential industries and the scarcity of lumber. Following the sharp curtailment of civilian furniture production, many furniture producers secured government contracts to make a wide variety of military supplies. It has been estimated that southern furniture manufacturers were awarded the bulk of these contracts because of their ability to turn out volume production at low cost.[131]

In addition to providing government contracts to the furniture industry, the war also reduced the industry's work force. Because of the draft and the attraction of higher wages in defense-related industries, many plants were forced to supplement their work forces by turning to previously underutilized sources of labor, primarily Negroes and women. This economic necessity proved particularly advantageous for Negroes, as it provided them with an opportunity to disprove on a large scale many of the derogatory opinions still commonly held concerning their abilities and industrial aptitude.

The end of the war did not bring a major displacement of Negro labor in the furniture industry. Because of strong consumer demands brought on by high wartime incomes, the furniture industry began to expand rapidly. Such expansion made it necessary not only to retain wartime-trained labor but also to employ large numbers of additional workers.

The South was in an excellent position to capitalize on the tremendous demand for furniture. Because many southern factories had stayed open during the war by filling government contracts, it was relatively easy for them to quickly shift to civilian production. In addition, southern producers had invested quite heavily in plants and equipment prior to the war, and so were able to turn out furniture faster than any other part of the country. As a result, by the mid-1940s, the Federal Reserve district office in Richmond, Virginia, announced that the Southeast had officially become the furniture-producing center of the country. In addition, North Carolina had overtaken New York as the nation's leading furniture state, producing at least 12 percent of the nation's total furniture output.[132]

---

131. Thomas, *op. cit.*, p. 73.

132. *Ibid.*, p. 76.

The combination of wartime work experience and the post-war expansion of the furniture industry seemed to insure that blacks would maintain their employment gains. Negroes hired during the war, in addition to being experienced workers and therefore particularly valuable in a time of expansion, had proven that blacks could perform well in furniture plants. Thus, whereas the war had provided Negroes with new opportunities, the postwar expansion ensured their retention and stimulated further hiring of Negroes.

Between 1940 and 1950 every region, particularly the South, increased its level of furniture employment and its level of Negro employment (Table 20). In fact, in every region the number of both Negroes and women employed increased by approximately 100 percent or more. By 1950 the level of Negro participation in the industry ranged from 2.4 percent in the West to 12.5 percent in the South, with the Northeast and the North Central states reporting 3.9 and 3.3 percent respectively. Table 16 shows that for the nation as a whole the total number of Negroes employed in furniture production more than doubled between 1940 and 1950, and the percentage of Negroes to all employees increased from 3.6 percent to 6.1 percent. In addition, the number of women in the furniture work force more than doubled while the number of Negro women increased by over 500 percent.

In contrast to the preceding decade, the 1950s brought real prosperity for the industry. With a rising standard of living, a housing boom, and the popularity of television and the ac-companying home-centered life style, furniture became the second largest durable goods industry in the nation.[133]

In this decade the South continued to outproduce all other regions. Between 1947 and 1956, the rate of growth for the southern furniture industry was over twice that of the nation as a whole. By the mid-1950s almost half of all wood bedroom furniture made in the United States came from within a 125-mile radius of High Point, North Carolina. In that area, companies such as Bassett, Stanley, American, Lane, Drexel, Broy-hill, and Thomasville had become giants in the industry.[134]

With this further concentration of the industry in the South, employment opportunities for Negroes continued to increase.

---

133. U.S. Department of Commerce, *The Furniture Industry and Its Potential Market* (Washington: U.S. Government Printing Office, 1950), p. 1.

134. Thomas, *op. cit.*, p. 87.

TABLE 20. *Furniture Industry*
Total Employment by Race, Sex, and Region, 1940-1960

	All Employees			Male			Female		
	Total	Negro	Percent Negro	Total	Negro	Percent Negro	Total	Negro	Percent Negro
Northeast									
1940	61,154	1,006	1.6	54,755	959	1.8	6,399	47	0.7
1950	86,201	3,378	3.9	73,324	2,929	4.0	12,877	449	3.5
1960	89,252	5,279	5.9	73,795	4,480	6.1	15,457	799	5.2
North Central									
1940	84,005	918	1.1	74,564	754	1.0	9,441	164	1.7
1950	115,744	3,861	3.3	95,132	2,974	3.1	20,612	887	4.3
1960	107,272	5,170	4.8	85,637	4,211	4.9	21,635	959	4.4
South									
1940	61,750	6,133	9.9	57,953	5,747	9.9	3,797	386	10.2
1950	96,577	12,100	12.5	83,601	10,171	12.2	12,976	1,929	14.9
1960	138,313	16,092	11.6	117,277	13,742	11.7	21,036	2,350	11.2
West									
1940	18,766	66	0.4	17,139	58	0.3	1,627	8	0.5
1950	31,721	777	2.4	26,817	674	2.5	4,904	103	2.1
1960	41,857	1,397	3.3	34,847	1,226	3.5	7,010	171	2.4

Sources: *U.S. Census of Population*
1940: Vol III, *The Labor Force, Part 1*, Table 77.
1950: Vol. II, *Characteristics of the Population, Part 1*, Table 161.
1960: *U.S. Summary*, PC(1)1D, Table 260.

Between 1950 and 1960 the number of Negroes employed nationwide increased from 20,430 to 28,845, or from 6.1 to 7.4 percent of total employment, thus illustrating the effect of combining a growth industry with the availability of Negro labor (Table 16). Approximately 47 percent of the 8,415 increase in Negro employment was attributable to the South. Because of the even greater expansion of total employment, however, Negroes as a percent of southern furniture employment declined from 12.5 percent in 1950 to 11.6 percent in 1960 (Table 20). Although the 1950s saw a continued increase in the employment of Negroes, it did not match the growth that had occurred in the previous decade. Nevertheless, the stage was set for the next decade, which would prove to be a period of major gains for the Negro in the furniture industry.

CHAPTER IV

Negro Employment in the 1960s

In 1961 Negro college students in the South began a series of sit-ins at public facilities, with the intention of arousing public awareness of discrimination. It is ironic that the first such sit-in took place in Greensboro, North Carolina—approximately 20 miles from High Point, the hub of the southern furniture industry. In spite of this early attention focused on conditions in the center of the furniture industry, the industry itself has been virtually ignored by those interested in furthering Negro employment opportunities. Even with this lack of attention, the industry experienced major increases in the employment of Negroes during the 1960s. As will be pointed out below, these gains of the 1960s, rather than being directly attributable to government pressure, were primarily the result of a labor market phenomenon.

THE FEDERAL GOVERNMENT AND EQUAL EMPLOYMENT OPPORTUNITY

Until the mid-1960s, government intervention into the area of civil rights was accomplished almost exclusively by means of presidential executive orders. President Franklin D. Roosevelt set the precedent in 1941 by issuing Executive Order 8802 establishing the President's Committee on Fair Employment Practices. Roosevelt's committee was followed by a succession of committees whose jurisdiction was limited to establishments doing business under contracts with the federal government. These committees were first set up by President Truman and then reorganized by each succeeding president.[135] In general, these committees have focused attention on industries other than furniture manufacturing. For example, President Eisenhower's Committee

---

135. Herbert R. Northrup and Gordon F. Bloom, *Economics of Labor Relations* (Homewood, Ill.: Richard D. Irwin, Inc., 1969), p. 706.

on Government Contracts, chaired by then vice president Richard M. Nixon, concentrated much of its equal opportunity efforts on the southern petroleum industry, but gave relatively little attention to other southern industries.

President John F. Kennedy's Committee on Equal Employment Opportunity (PCEEO), established in 1961 by Executive Order 10925, brought increased pressures on certain portions of American industry. By threatening to cancel contracts of noncompliance companies the committee had a definite impact on such employers as southern steel manufacturers. Again, however, the furniture industry escaped close scrutiny.

Legislation and Government Organizations

President Lyndon B. Johnson issued Executive Order 11246, which established the Office of Federal Contract Compliance (OFCC). During Johnson's administration the Civil Rights Act of 1964, creating the Equal Employment Opportunity Commission (EEOC), was passed. At present these two agencies continue to be directly involved in equal employment matters, reporting to the secretary of labor and the president, respectively. Again, however, the furniture industry has continued to avoid equal employment pressures from the government.

The lack of current pressures may be explained in part by two factors. First, the industry has employed blacks since the turn of the century. Although the level of Negro employment has not always been high, it has increased from decade to decade, with major gains occurring during the 1960s. Second, until recently most furniture plants were outside the jurisdiction of the OFCC and EEOC. Since many companies do not contract with the government and those that do are involved in relatively small measure, they are generally beyond the power of OFCC. In addition, most furniture plants were also excluded from EEOC coverage by virtue of their size. In 1967, when Title VII of the Civil Rights Act became effective, it applied only to employers with 100 or more employees. After periodic adjustments, coverage was extended by the 1972 amendment to employers with 15 or more employees. Given the small size of the average furniture plant, it was thus only recently that EEOC jurisdiction encompassed many of them.

EEOC DATA AND THEIR LIMITATIONS

The basic data utilized herein, for analysis of black employment progress during the 1960s, as in other studies in this series, are those provided by the Equal Employment Opportunity Commission. It is necessary to note, however, that comparisons between EEOC data and those published by the U. S. Bureau of the Census, which were used as our basic data for 1960 and previous years, must always be handled with care, since different methods of data collection are used by each organization. Census data are based on responses of individuals to Bureau of the Census interrogators or questionnaires, whereas EEOC data are compiled from reports submitted by employers. Since individuals are often likely to perceive their employment status as being different from what employer records would indicate, this in itself would likely result in some differences in the racial composition of the industry's work force as reported by EEOC and census data.

More significant for the furniture industry, however, is the reporting requirement of Title VII of the Civil Rights Act of 1964. Even though this Act currently applies to all employers of 15 or more employees who meet other coverage requirements of the Act, only those employing 100 or more workers must submit employment data. In 1967, the furniture industry reported that only 960 out of 10,008 plants employed 100 or more workers, and only 3,449—approximately one-third—employed 20 or more workers.[136] Some of these plants were, of course, owned by companies which had a total labor force in excess of 100 employees, and would thereby be required to file reports with EEOC, and others may have by now expanded sufficiently to come within the reporting requirement. Nevertheless, it is obvious that the vast majority of all furniture plants are not represented in EEOC data.

Because the larger furniture plants employ more than 50 percent of the industry's labor force, the EEOC data since 1966 include more than one-half of all furniture workers. Our findings, however, are that the EEOC data overstate the percentages of Negroes in the industry, because larger firms tend to employ higher percentages of Negroes. There are several reasons for this. First, larger firms have greater public visibility and therefore are generally more susceptible to public pressures to be an

---

136. U.S. Bureau of the Census, *Census of Manufactures, 1967:* Vol. II, *Industry Statistics,* pp. 25-27.

equal opportunity employer. Second, the larger furniture plants tend to be more heavily concentrated in the South and are therefore able to draw on a larger supply of Negro labor. This contention is supported by the fact that in 1969 slightly more than 50 percent of total United States furniture employment reported in the EEOC survey was located in the South, although only 44 percent of the total number of reporting establishments were found there. Third, small southern firms located in the South tend to be concentrated in such areas as rural Western North Carolina or Eastern Tennessee, where few Negroes dwell, while the larger firms have plants in more urbanized areas where the percentage of blacks is much higher. Finally, many of the smaller furniture companies are staffed almost entirely by relatives, friends, and neighbors of the proprietor, thereby making a racial mixture unlikely.

Initial 1970 data supplied by the U.S. Bureau of the Census for key furniture states support these conclusions. Table 21 compares census and EEOC data by race and sex for the top ten states in terms of furniture industry employment.

The hypothesis that census data tend to reflect lower employment percentages for Negroes than do EEOC data is supported by seven of the ten states listed in Table 21. Only in Ohio, New York, and Indiana does the hypothesis not hold true, and even here the variation ranges from only 0.0 to 0.5 percentage points. The variations in Ohio and Indiana are no doubt explained by the relatively low number of Negroes reported as employed in furniture. Such a low number could easily cause slight sampling errors to become quite significant. The variation in New York is possibly attributable to the relatively large number of blacks who are employed in the very small furniture assembly operations of New York City. It is possible that in New York City, in contrast to the country as a whole, the small shops employ a larger percentage of Negroes than do larger ones.

THE OVERALL PICTURE, 1960-1970

Despite the limitations of the EEOC data, there can be no doubt that, during the 1960s, the percentage of Negro participation in the furniture industry almost doubled. Most of this increase occurred in the latter half of the decade. In 1960 the U. S. Census reported that 7.4 percent of the 376,694 furniture employees were Negroes (see Chapter III). Data supplied to

TABLE 21. Furniture Industry
Employment by Race and Sex
A Comparison of Census and EEOC Data for the Ten Major Employment States, 1970

States		All Employees			Male			Female		
		Total	Negro	Percent Negro	Total	Negro	Percent Negro	Total	Negro	Percent Negro
California	Census	34,440	1,734	5.0	27,432	1,490	5.4	7,008	244	3.5
	EEOC	12,252	1,087	8.9	9,585	914	9.5	2,667	173	6.5
Illinois	Census	21,253	2,507	11.8	15,415	1,741	11.3	5,838	766	13.1
	EEOC	13,801	2,220	16.1	9,887	1,614	16.3	3,914	606	15.5
Indiana	Census	21,512	480	2.2	14,123	262	1.9	7,389	218	3.0
	EEOC	16,657	284	1.7	11,487	151	1.3	5,170	133	2.6
Michigan	Census	21,057	1,003	4.8	15,584	632	4.1	5,473	371	6.8
	EEOC	15,935	911	5.7	12,078	602	5.0	3,857	309	8.0
New York	Census	28,037	2,283	8.1	22,356	1,867	8.4	5,681	416	7.3
	EEOC	13,207	1,018	7.7	9,975	767	7.7	3,232	251	7.8
North Carolina	Census	62,882	7,621	12.1	45,387	4,804	10.6	17,495	2,817	16.1
	EEOC	53,578	7,713	14.4	39,023	5,059	13.0	14,555	2,654	18.2
Ohio	Census	16,952	1,112	6.6	13,107	878	6.7	3,845	234	6.1
	EEOC	10,428	685	6.6	7,818	538	6.9	2,610	147	5.6
Pennsylvania	Census	25,591	1,409	5.5	20,054	1,130	5.6	5,537	279	5.0
	EEOC	16,516	1,063	6.4	12,548	897	7.1	3,968	166	4.2
Tennessee	Census	20,727	2,287	11.0	15,293	1,441	9.4	5,434	846	15.6
	EEOC	16,384	2,357	14.4	11,923	1,494	12.5	4,461	863	19.3
Virginia	Census	22,249	4,983	22.4	16,214	3,212	19.8	6,035	1,771	29.3
	EEOC	20,455	5,146	25.2	15,010	3,465	23.1	5,445	1,681	30.9

Sources: *U.S. Census of Population: 1970, Detailed Characteristics*, Series PC(1)D, Table 184 for each state; and U.S. Equal Employment Opportunity Commission, 1970.

TABLE 22. Furniture Industry
Percent Negro Employment by Sex and Occupational Group
United States, 1964-1970

Occupational Group	All Employees					Male					Female				
	1964	1966	1967	1969	1970	1964	1966	1967	1969	1970	1964	1966	1967	1969	1970
Officials and managers	0.4	0.5	0.7	1.1	1.4	0.3	0.5	0.7	1.1	1.4	2.1	0.4	0.6	1.7	2.4
Professionals	0.3	0.6	0.7	0.5	0.7	0.3	0.7	0.7	0.4	0.6	—	—	0.6	1.5	1.6
Technicians	0.5	0.9	1.2	1.5	1.6	0.5	0.9	1.2	1.5	1.6	—	0.6	1.2	1.4	2.0
Sales workers	—	*	0.1	0.3	0.3	—	*	0.1	0.2	0.2	—	—	—	1.6	1.9
Office and clerical workers	1.4	1.6	2.0	2.5	2.5	2.0	3.0	4.0	4.1	4.2	1.1	1.1	1.4	2.0	2.0
Total white collar	0.8	1.0	1.2	1.6	1.7	0.6	0.9	1.2	1.4	1.5	1.0	1.1	1.3	1.9	2.0
Craftsmen	4.0	6.1	7.0	8.9	8.9	3.9	6.1	7.1	8.6	8.6	6.1	5.3	6.5	10.5	11.4
Operatives	9.3	12.7	13.9	15.7	15.5	9.3	12.9	14.2	15.6	15.3	9.6	11.5	12.7	16.1	16.2
Laborers	7.3	21.4	22.8	21.4	21.8	7.5	21.8	22.8	22.5	22.5	6.7	20.3	22.8	19.1	20.5
Service workers	22.5	24.3	24.2	24.6	23.0	21.7	23.5	23.8	23.5	22.0	29.2	33.3	28.7	32.4	31.6
Total blue collar	8.0	13.8	15.1	16.1	15.9	7.9	13.8	14.8	15.8	15.4	8.6	14.0	15.9	16.9	17.4
Total	6.4	11.5	12.7	13.4	13.2	6.6	11.9	12.9	13.5	13.0	5.4	10.1	12.1	13.3	13.8

Sources: Appendix Tables A-1 to A-5.

Note: 1964:   105 establishments.
        1966:   978 establishments.
        1967: 1,092 establishments.
        1969: 1,139 establishments.
        1970: 1,170 establishments.

* Less than 0.05 percent.

the President's Committee on Equal Employment Opportunity [137] in 1964 indicated that the level of Negro employment was approximately 6.4 percent; by 1969 EEOC data recorded a level of 13.4 percent (Table 22).   Since the 1964 data were based on a nonrandom survey of only 105 out of more than 10,000 plants, their reliability is questionable.   Nevertheless, the indication is that the first half of the 1960s saw very little gain, if any, in terms of the level of Negro employment.

By 1966, EEOC data, drawn from employers of 100 or more employees, were estimating that the level of Negro employment had increased sharply, to 11.5 percent.   As might be expected, virtually all of the increase occurred in the blue collar job categories, with principal gains occurring in the laborer category. Between 1966 and 1969 the level of Negro employment continued to increase.   Again, this was particularly true of employment in blue collar jobs, as the levels rose from 13.8 percent to 16.1 percent.   Only in 1970 was there even a slight decline in the percentage.

White collar jobs also began to open up somewhat after 1966. With a gradual increase each year, the level of Negro employment in white collar jobs more than doubled between 1964 and 1970.   It still, however, remains an area of low representation for Negroes, as only 1.7 percent of 51,365 white collar jobs reported in 1970 by EEOC were held by Negroes.

The Labor Market Phenomenon

As mentioned earlier, the expansion of Negro employment, particularly blue collar employment, has been largely a labor market phenomenon.   This phenomenon, as in the paper-converting and textile industries,[138] seems to have been created by locational factors in combination with a low-skill, growth industry.   As discussed in Chapter II, the furniture industry is heavily dependent on semiskilled and unskilled labor.   In addition, it is a low-paying industry that has continued to grow at a substantial rate. Therefore, the industry is required to utilize whatever labor is available.   Since the industry is heavily concentrated in the South, where there is a large supply of black labor and where many white male workers have, especially more recently, been

---

137. The President's Committee on Equal Employment Opportunity was the predecessor of the present Office of Federal Contract Compliance. The data provided by the PCEEO are much less inclusive than those of the EEOC.

138. See Northrup and Rowan, *Southern Industry, op. cit.*

able to find employment in better-paying industries, furniture manufacturers have had little choice but to employ increasing numbers of blacks and/or women.

It is not surprising that little gain occurred in the level of Negro employment during the early years of the 1960s, since relatively little gain occurred in total industry employment. By the beginning of 1964 total employment had increased by only approximately 19,000 [139] over the 1960 census figure of 375,497; therefore, Negroes had limited opportunities for improving their employment level.

Between 1964 and 1966 industry employment increased by approximately 70,000,[140] as the economy became more prosperous. To satisfy the industry's demand for labor, more and more blacks began to be employed (Table 22). With the continued expansion of industry employment into 1969, the level of Negro employment continued to increase. Only in 1970, when the level of total industry employment declined, did the level of Negro employment decline.

Another indication of the effect of economic forces on the furniture work force is seen by examining the changing figures for total employment for employers of 100 or more workers (Appendix Tables A-2 to A-5). Between the years of 1966 and 1970 total employment increased by 11,257. This increase, however, was the result of an increase of 21,324 women, which offset a decline of 10,067 men. Over half of this 11,257 increase consisted of Negroes, with 4,826 being women and 1,023 being men. Thus, it seems quite likely that for the near future the furniture work force may become increasingly dependent upon blacks and women as white male labor continues to be drawn away.

Because of general economic conditions, it is quite possible that black male labor will begin to be drawn away also, placing an even greater dependency on women of all races. Between 1969 and 1970 Negro male employment, based on EEOC figures, declined for the first time since at least 1964. This occurred despite the fact that total female and total Negro female employment continued to increase. More specifically, as total female and Negro female employment were increasing by approximately 3 percent and 6 percent respectively, total male and Negro male employment were declining by approximately 5 percent and 8 percent. Between the years of 1966 and 1970 the level of total

---

139. *Employment and Earnings*, March 1964, Table B-5.

140. *Ibid.*, March 1967, Table B-5.

women and Negro women in the work force increased from 20 percent and 2 percent, respectively, to 27 percent and 4 percent.

The Effect of Government Policy

Although economic factors were the major contributors to the increasing level of Negro employment in the furniture industry of the 1960s, they were not so effective at upgrading Negroes into higher job classifications. It is in the area of upgrading that government interests have made their greatest contribution. Because government policy has noted the underutilization of blacks in higher-ranking jobs throughout American industry, many furniture companies interviewed for this study report an increasing awareness of their deficiencies in this area and have begun correcting the situation.

As will be discussed later in greater detail, Negroes in the furniture industry have begun to be upgraded in recent years. Whereas in 1966, 98.5 percent of all Negroes employed in furniture companies of 100 or more employees were found in blue collar jobs, with 85.9 percent of the total employed as operatives or laborers, by 1970 the levels had declined slightly to 97.5 percent and 82.8 percent, respectively (Table 23). Most of this change seems to be the result of upgrading Negroes from laborers to operatives and craftsmen, with a few being placed in white collar jobs.

NATIONAL OCCUPATIONAL DISTRIBUTION

Employment in the furniture industry is heavily concentrated in the blue collar jobs, particularly in the unskilled and semi-skilled areas. More than four out of every five employees are in blue collar jobs and more than twenty-four out of every twenty-five black employees are in such jobs (Table 23). Although there has been a gradual reduction over the past few years in the proportion of jobs designated as blue collar, this category continues to remain the dominant area of employment for all applicants.

Officials and Managers [141]

Although there are relatively few Negroes in this category, it is nevertheless the second largest white collar category for

---

141. Data cited below for occupational distribution of blacks in each job category is taken from Appendix Tables A-2 to A-5.

TABLE 23. Furniture Industry
Occupational Distribution of Negroes and All Employees, by Percent
United States, 1964-1970

Occupational Group	All Employees					Negro Employees				
	1964	1966	1967	1969	1970	1964	1966	1967	1969	1970
Officials and managers	5.3	6.0	5.9	6.4	6.9	0.3	0.3	0.3	0.5	0.7
Professionals	1.7	1.2	0.9	1.0	1.2	0.1	0.1	0.1	*	0.1
Technicians	2.0	1.1	1.2	1.4	1.5	0.1	0.1	0.1	0.2	0.2
Sales workers	3.4	2.0	1.9	2.1	2.0	—	*	*	*	*
Office and clerical workers	10.3	7.6	7.2	7.4	7.4	2.2	1.0	1.2	1.4	1.4
Total white collar	22.7	17.9	17.1	18.3	19.0	2.7	1.5	1.7	2.1	2.4
Craftsmen	14.1	18.0	17.8	17.4	17.8	8.8	9.4	9.9	11.5	12.1
Operatives	38.4	40.2	40.7	38.8	39.6	56.0	44.2	44.5	45.4	46.6
Laborers	23.1	22.4	22.9	23.9	22.0	26.6	41.7	41.0	38.1	36.2
Service workers	1.7	1.5	1.5	1.6	1.6	5.9	3.2	2.9	2.9	2.7
Total blue collar	77.3	82.1	82.9	81.7	81.0	97.3	98.5	98.3	97.9	97.5
Total	100.0	100.0	100.0	100.0	100.0	100.0	100.0	100.0	100.0	100.0

Sources: Appendix Tables A-1 to A-5.

* Less than 0.05 percent.

Negro employment. In spite of the relatively low level of black participation, there has been a gradual increase since 1964. Whereas the 1964 data reported only 0.4 percent of the employees in this category as being Negroes, by 1970, 1.4 percent were Negroes. Although the percentage change among black women appears more impressive than the change occurring among black men, this is the result of the small number of female officials and managers.

There is little doubt but that a conscious effort to upgrade Negroes is occurring among some furniture manufacturers. In interviews with industry representatives, particularly in the South, it was not unusual for them to admit that they had employed very few blacks, if any, in this category until the last few years. They were now, however, actively looking for Negroes capable of being promoted. Almost all of the Negroes being promoted into this category are being done so via the foreman's route. The effects of such efforts are beginning to be seen.

Between 1966 and 1970, employment in the officials and managers category for firms with 100 or more employees increased from 15,547 to 18,652. Of this 3,105 increase, 5.8 percent were Negroes. If this increase is examined on a year-by-year basis, the results are even more encouraging for blacks. Between 1966 and 1967 the total number of officials and managers increased by 963; 3.8 percent of these were Negroes. In the period from 1967 to 1969 Negroes accounted for 5.9 percent of all those entering this category, and from 1969 to 1970 the figure was 8.3 percent. This last figure is particularly important since 1970 was a relatively depressed year for the furniture industry.

It seems quite obvious that past discrimination has been a factor in the low level of Negro employment in the officials and managers category. Although lack of skills on the part of many Negroes may have contributed substantially to their low level of usage, it seems unlikely that out of 35,656 Negro employees reported in 1970 by the EEOC survey, only 263 were capable of handling official and managerial responsibilities. This past discrimination, however, is beginning to change as more companies become aware of the problem and as more plants become increasingly black in work force composition.

The location of many furniture plants has also worked against the employment of more Negro managers. In states outside the South many plants are located in areas of low Negro population.

In the South, the industry is heavily concentrated in small rural towns, where Negroes with managerial ability are often very reluctant to settle. Thus, if Negroes are to make substantial employment gains in the officials and managers category in the near future, it will have to be done primarily through promotions into foremen's jobs, as is currently taking place.

Professionals and Technicians

Professional and technical jobs in the furniture industry are quite rare. In fact these two categories are the smallest found in furniture employment, reporting in 1970 only 1.2 percent and 1.5 percent of total employment respectively. This low level is to be understood in light of the small size of most furniture companies. One would not expect to find very many professionals or technicians, if any, in approximately two-thirds of the companies, since these employ twenty or fewer workers.

When the lack of jobs in the professional category is combined with the difficulty of finding trained Negroes willing to reside in furniture areas and the difficulty of competing for professional talent with higher-paying industries, it is not surprising that very few Negroes are found in the professional jobs of the furniture industry. As of 1970, only twenty-one Negroes were found in this category and this level had increased by only one since 1966. As an indication of the lack of opportunity, the total number of professional employees in the industry, as reported by EEOC, increased by only fifteen from 1966 to 1970 in spite of the addition of 192 plants to the survey. Although between 1966 and 1970 the number of men employed as professionals declined, as did the number of Negro men, the number of women and Negro women increased but remained at a very low level.

Since no research and development work and little if any design innovation are done by any but the larger companies in the industry, it is not surprising that technicians are relatively unused by the furniture industry. Although there has been a gradual increase over the past few years in the number of such employees, it still represents the second smallest category of employment for the industry. In spite of the fact that it is an area of limited employment potential, it has proved to be one of the first white collar jobs into which blacks have been promoted. It was not uncommon for some firms in the mid-1960s to report the employment of a Negro technician before there were blacks in any other nonclerical white collar job. In some cases this was accomplished either by personally encouraging a promising black employee to acquire technical training on his own or occasionally encouraging him to take advantage of company-sponsored or subsidized training programs.[142] Such efforts on the part of most furniture manufacturers appear to be quite limited.

In general, the professional and technical positions of the furniture industry remain areas of underutilization for the black employee. Although some advancement is occurring, particularly in the technical category, increased employment of Negroes in these categories continues to be hampered by the fact that these jobs employ a small number of people and that those Negroes who possess the necessary skills are often drawn away from areas of furniture production or are attracted to higher-paying industries in these areas. The situation is further affected by the relative lack of active recruitment of blacks for such positions. Particularly in the South, where there are a number of predominately Negro colleges, it would seem that active recruitment could produce some greater results in these categories.

Sales Workers

Many racial policy studies of other American industries support the fact that Negroes suffer the greatest discrimination in seeking employment in sales positions. Furniture manufacturing is certainly no exception. Although approximately 2.0 percent of the furniture work force is employed in a selling capacity, as late as 1970 less than 0.05 percent of the Negroes working in furniture were so employed. As low as this level is, there has been some recent progress in the employment of black sales personnel. For example, in 1966 there were only two Negroes reported in the entire EEOC national survey as being sales workers; both of them were men. By 1967 the number had increased by only one. Within two years, however, an additional seven women and six men had been employed. By 1970 the total number was increased to seventeen by the hiring of an additional woman, in spite of the fact that the number of total sales workers declined by 291. Even though the number of black sales workers increased by over 500 percent within two years, Negroes currently represent only 0.3 percent of total sales personnel.

---

142. Interview, December 1971.

Furniture sales personnel are almost exclusively involved in selling to retailers, not directly to the public. Such sales are generally accomplished either by calling directly on the retailer or by servicing a manufacturer's display at a national or regional furniture market such as High Point or Chicago. In recent years some of the larger manufacturers have built permanent display facilities where sales personnel man the operation on a continuing basis. Since the furniture industry is an extremely competitive industry with relatively little manufacturer identification by the consumer, it has been important to many manufacturers that they not run the risk of alienating a potential retailer of their product by use of a Negro sales person. Thus, the limited use of Negro sales workers is as much a reflection upon a society whose purchases may be affected by the race of a salesman as it is upon the furniture manufacturer who must appease the purchaser if he is to compete successfully.

From the slight changes that have already taken place in the racial makeup of furniture manufacturers' sales forces and from interviews with industry representatives, it seems likely that an increasing number of Negro sales workers will be employed in the industry. As the attitudes of the public have changed, some companies have already begun actively looking for Negro sales personnel. It still seems, however, that for a long time to come blacks will be underemployed in this category.

Office and Clerical Workers

The largest white collar category for total employment as well as for Negro employment is that of clericals. It is through this classification that blacks seem most often to enter the white collar area. It has generally been considered easier to hire Negro secretarial help or to upgrade a Negro blue collar worker to a position as a shipping clerk than to employ Negroes in other white collar positions. Thus, often before a company hires its first black professional or promotes its first black foreman, a first is likely to occur in the office and clerical category.

Occasionally the hiring of a Negro secretary has been done by the personnel office of a company as a symbol to both white and black employees and applicants that it is committed to equal employment opportunities. One executive for a major southern manufacturer indicated that shortly after the passage of the Civil Rights Act he employed a Negro receptionist for his own office. He felt that by employing her he could not only demonstrate to some company personnel that Negroes were capable of performing well in such jobs but could also prove to applicants, particularly Negro applicants, that his company was indeed an equal opportunity employer. Not only has such a decision encouraged applicants for blue collar jobs but it has also enabled him to employ additional Negroes in white collar positions. Whereas in 1967 he had only one Negro so employed, by 1971 there were eighteen Negroes, as well as some other minorities, employed in white collar jobs.[143]

As would be expected, the clerical category consists largely of women, and in fact the number of men, as reported by the EEOC, has declined consistently since 1966. In spite of this decline in the number of men, Negro men have increased their overall level since 1966, although the number declined somewhat in 1970. As this has been occurring, the number of Negro women employed in clerical positions has almost doubled, and as of 1970 was at a high of 313.

In general, office and clerical positions in many companies have offered Negroes white collar employment when they were unable to find it in other categories. Except for a stabilization of the level in 1970, the level of Negroes in this category has constantly increased until it has reached a high of 2.5 percent of all clerical employees.

Craftsmen

Although the furniture industry is heavily dependent upon unskilled and semiskilled workers, the more skilled positions do represent a sizable percentage of industry jobs, approximately 18 percent, making it the third largest category in the industry and roughly equivalent to total employment in the white collar jobs. Included in this category would be such workers as upholsterers, carpenters, electricians, mechanics, repairmen, pattern makers and some leadmen. Since most furniture plants, and particularly the larger ones, are located in small towns in the more rural portions of the country, it is essential that they retain a maintenance force rather than rely on independent sources in the community. To generate a source of craftsmen for their plants, some companies have been willing to develop internal training programs, encourage local high schools to develop furniture-oriented vocational training programs, and participate in

---

143. Interview, January 1972.

community programs designed to train the unemployed. Such projects have sometimes been undertaken with the objective not only of securing additional trained employees but also of providing a source of training and employment for blacks.

The number of blacks employed as craftsmen has increased appreciably in the latter half of the 1960s. Whereas in 1964, according to a limited EEOC survey, Negroes represented 4.0 percent of craftsmen employed, by 1969 the level had increased to 8.9 percent, and remained the same for 1970. Although the total number of craftsmen declined by 1,582 from 1967 to 1970, the number of Negro craftsmen increased by 800. As in the case of office and clerical personnel, both the total number of men and the number of black men in this category have declined slightly in the last year or two, although women, and particularly Negro women, have shown impressive gains. For example, from 1969 to 1970 the number of total male and Negro male craftsmen declined by 877 and 111 respectively, while the figures for all women and Negro women were increasing by 732 and 132 respectively. In 1970 there was a combined total of 4,292 Negroes employed as craftsmen in the furniture companies of 100 or more workers.

Although women have made quite dramatic gains in employment as craftsmen, it still continues to be a heavily male-oriented category, with more than four out of every five jobs being filled by men. If the trend toward the employment of women in this industry continues, it can be expected that all job categories, including the craftsmen category, will become increasingly composed of women.

In most industries the more skilled jobs imply an appreciably higher wage rate. However, because of the common use of incentive systems, this is not always the case in furniture plants. As an example, one upholstery plant reported that although their upholsterers were paid quite well, a cushion stuffer was the highest-paid production worker.[144] Thus, in some plants, because of the prevalence of incentive pay systems, there may not be the financial incentive for Negroes to move from semiskilled jobs to the more skilled ones. Nevertheless, on a national scale there has been an upward movement of blacks from the semiskilled and unskilled jobs into the more skilled positions.

------

144. Interview, April 1972.

Operatives

The employees who operate the various pieces of machinery in the plants are the backbone of the furniture industry. Approximately 40 percent of all furniture personnel are employed to operate such pieces of equipment as electric saws, lathes, and sanders. Although the machinery is essential to these operations, much of the work has to be done by hand, as the operator must personally maneuver the unfinished piece of furniture and/or the piece of equipment so that the raw material receives the appropriate treatment. In many case-goods plants the operation has remained unchanged for the past quarter of a century or longer, except for the occasional addition of a conveyor belt. Upholstery operations are no more advanced. According to one industrial relations executive, the last major advance in automating the upholstery operation was the introduction of the staple gun.[145]

Since World War II machine-operating jobs have been a major source of Negro employment. Because the level of the work required is semiskilled at best, Negroes have not come up against the barriers to employment that existed in some of the more skilled positions. Consequently, the level of black employment has continued to rise. In 1970, almost half of all blacks employed in furniture-manufacturing companies of 100 or more workers were employed as operatives. Having reached a high in 1969 of 16,944, or 15.7 percent of operative employment, the level of blacks in this category dropped slightly in 1970 to 16,614, or 15.5 percent. Again, as was the case among craftsmen, the number of men has been declining since 1967, with the numbers of Negro men declining slightly from 1969 to 1970, while both the total number of women and the number of Negro women have increased continually. From 1966 to 1970 the number of women employed as operatives increased by more than 40 percent to 27,498 and the number of Negro women increased by approximately 118 percent to 4,445.

As the furniture industry has expanded over the past decade, Negroes have been able to find increasing employment opportunities as equipment operators. Industry expansion and the exodus of many white male operatives have made necessary the employment of large numbers of Negroes. In the last year or so there appears to be a slight exodus of Negro men, perhaps to

---

145. Interview, April 1972.

other industries, thus causing furniture manufacturers to turn increasingly to women, both black and white. Because an employee hired as a machine operator often remains such throughout his term of employment, and because the work environment is often noisy and dusty and the pay relatively low, it is not surprising that a sizable number of employees are attracted to other nearby industries.

Laborers

Slightly more than one out of every five furniture employees is classified as a laborer; this category is the second largest source of employment for all employees as well as for all Negro employees in the industry. Such workers are generally unskilled and perform such tasks as lifting and loading raw materials and finished products. They are quite frequently employed in such areas as the lumber yards, the packing and shipping departments, and the production area, where they are used to move work in process from one station to another.

In the early days of the industry this was the area in which blacks found their greatest employment opportunities. As of 1970, 36.2 percent of all Negroes in furniture companies employing 100 or more workers were employed as laborers. As high as this level is, it does represent a gradual decrease in recent years as Negroes have been upgraded into more skilled jobs. In spite of this upward movement of Negro employment, Negroes continue to make up slightly more than 21 percent of all laborers—a level that has remained relatively constant since 1966.

As in all other blue collar jobs, the number of men employed as laborers has declined since 1967—a decline of 8,002. In addition, the number of Negro men in this category has declined substantially, from 10,576 to 8,629. Although some of this decline was no doubt due to economic conditions, particularly in 1970, a more important factor would appear to be the continuation of the exodus of male labor from furniture manufacturing. Total female employment and total Negro female employment in this area have continued to increase over the same period of time; however, total female employment did drop slightly in 1970 while Negro female employment rose slightly. As in other blue collar categories, male labor continues to dominate this area; men hold approximately 65 percent of all laborer jobs. This level, however, has dropped from approximately 78 percent in less than five years, thus highlighting a trend that seems to be occurring in most blue collar positions.

Service Workers

This category consists primarily of nonproduction-related positions, such as janitor. Consequently, it represents a very small proportion of furniture employment for Negroes as well as all employees. Although Negroes generally make up 23 to 25 percent of all service workers, by 1970 such jobs represented only 2.7 percent of total Negro employment, a level which represents a gradual decrease since the middle of the 1960s.

Contrary to the situation in other blue collar jobs, both total male and Negro male employment either increased or remained relatively stable from 1966 to 1969. Such a situation also occurred in total female and Negro female employment. In 1970, with the depressed economic conditions, all service categories for the larger firms declined in the number of employees, with the major decline occurring among Negro employees, both men and women. Of the 193 jobs eliminated, 111 had been held by Negroes, leaving a total of 4,200 service workers and 968 Negro service workers.

Household Furniture vs. Office Furniture

As discussed in Chapter II, more than two-thirds of total furniture employment is to be found in the household furniture sector rather than the office furniture sector. When the relative standing of these two sectors is compared in regard to the employment of Negroes, it is seen that this employment concentration works to their advantage. Household furniture employed a higher percentage of Negroes in almost every job category in both 1964 and 1969 (Table 24). Rather than being the result of a greater reluctance on the part of office furniture manufacturers to employ blacks, it seems likely that the distinction is based on population characteristics. As discussed earlier, office furniture production tends to be more heavily concentrated in the nonsouthern areas, whereas household furniture production is heavily concentrated in the South. Thus, the relative availability of Negro labor seems a more reasonable explanation of the difference than does employment discrimination. The most important point to be gained by a comparison of the two sectors is that both report substantial improvements

TABLE 24. Furniture Industry
Percent Negro Employment by Occupational Group
Total Industry and Household and Office Furniture Plants
United States, 1964 and 1969

Occupational Group	(25) Total Industry		(251) Household Furniture		(252) Office Furniture	
	1964	1969	1964	1969	1964	1969
Officials and managers	0.4	1.1	0.6	1.2	0.3	1.1
Professionals	0.3	0.5	0.6	0.5	—	0.9
Technicians	0.5	1.5	—	1.6	—	0.9
Sales workers	—	0.3	—	0.3	—	0.2
Office and clerical workers	1.4	2.5	2.2	2.7	0.8	1.4
Total white collar	0.8	1.6	1.3	1.7	0.4	1.1
Craftsmen	4.0	8.9	4.9	9.3	4.2	10.5
Operatives	9.3	15.7	11.9	17.3	7.7	10.6
Laborers	7.3	21.4	7.7	23.6	8.1	14.2
Service workers	22.5	24.6	32.3	27.3	21.5	17.9
Total blue collar	8.0	16.1	9.6	17.6	7.6	11.6
Total	6.4	13.4	8.2	15.1	5.4	9.2

Sources: 1964: Data in author's possession.
1969: U.S. Equal Employment Opportunity Commission.

in the level of Negro employment in blue collar jobs, particularly in the more skilled jobs, and some improvement in almost all white collar jobs.

INTRAPLANT MOVEMENT OF WORKERS

The intraplant movement of furniture workers is generally quite limited. Although skill barriers do not present much of a problem, the structure of the industry provides little incentive for employee mobility.

Comparable to the situation in the textile industry, when progression occurs in the blue collar areas it is normally from unskilled to semiskilled to skilled jobs.[146] It is, however, not unusual for an employee to be hired directly as a semiskilled operator and remain such throughout his term of employment. Since the operative category accounts for approximately 40 percent of all industry personnel, and approximately two-thirds of the industry's jobs are at or below the level of operatives, there is not the room for upward mobility that is found in other areas, such as the aerospace industry or even paper mills.[147] In addition, there is no strong financial incentive for upward progression. Because of the common use of incentive systems and base wage rates that do not vary greatly from department to department, it is not unusual for relatively unskilled workers to make as much as or occasionally even more than more skilled workers.

Employment in white collar jobs is generally direct. Although a capable blue collar employee may be promoted to a foreman's position or to a clerical position, most white collar jobs are filled by hiring from the outside. This is particularly true for professionals and members of management. As indicated earlier, many of the top management positions are filled by relatives of the owner.

UNION POLICY

As discussed earlier, union organization of the furniture industry has enjoyed only limited success. Consequently, unions have had little impact on the distribution of manpower within the industry or on the intraplant movement of labor. In recent years, however, at least two trends have developed which many industry people feel may stimulate further organizing success.

---

146. See Rowan, *op. cit.*, p. 78.

147. See Northrup, *Southern Industry, op. cit.* and *Basic Industry, op. cit.*

First, the increasing level of black employment is seen as likely to bring on greater unionization. Almost every industry representative interviewed, both in and out of the South, expressed the view that the increasing level of black employment was likely to have such a result. Even some representatives of industry unions agreed with such views. If the textile industry is any indication, these views may be unsupportable. In recent years the textile industry has become increasingly black in the composition of its work force,[148] and yet has retained a relatively nonunionized status.

A second trend is the entry of conglomerates into the industry in recent years, a trend which is seen by some as a potential source of union success. Although fears that conglomerates might be less willing to resist unions have subsided somewhat, there does seem to be a greater propensity for the purchased company to become the target of a union organizing campaign. Unions already having established a bargaining relationship with the parent organization seem particularly quick to respond.

It seems unlikely that any increased union success in the furniture industry will greatly affect the intraplant movement of personnel. Even though formal seniority systems may become more common, the industry structure will no doubt continue to be the controlling factor. Thus, the abundance of labor concentrated in relatively comparable skill levels and wage classifications will continue to affect the upward mobility of labor. In addition, it is not unusual for nonunion plants to maintain a seniority system of their own.

SUMMARY OF THE DECADE

Although the great emphasis placed on the area of civil rights in the 1960s has no doubt contributed to the increased employment of Negroes in the furniture industry, it seems quite likely that the economic forces of supply and demand have been the major catalysts. Because of the relatively low level of skill required for most furniture production jobs, manufacturers have been able to utilize, in almost all blue collar areas, what previously might have been considered marginal workers. This lack of required skill, combined with a growing demand for labor and the availability of Negroes, created the foundation for increased employment of Negroes. These economic factors will be discussed in greater detail in the following chapter.

---

148. See Rowan, *op. cit.*

CHAPTER V

Regional Employment Patterns, 1960-1970[149]

Although furniture manufacturing is found in every state of this country, there is substantial variation in terms of total employment among regions and states. This variation is particularly notable for Negro employment (Tables 25 and 26). In this chapter primary attention will be given to the hypothesis that for the furniture industry, locational factors, especially population characteristics, are the dominant influence affecting Negro employment.

An examination of EEOC data for the employment of Negroes in the furniture industry in 1969 shows a regional range from 1.1 percent of total workers in New England, where Negro population percentages are the lowest, to 19.6 percent of total workers in the South, where Negro population percentages are the highest. The fact that a region has a high level of total Negro employment, however, is no assurance that high levels will prevail in all job categories. In order to examine employment variations more closely, each major region will be considered separately.

NEW ENGLAND

The region where the American furniture industry began and was concentrated during the first years of its history had 21,400 employees, or only 4.7 percent of the total furniture work

---

149. All references to 1960 population and furniture data in this chapter are based on the *U.S. Census of Population, 1960: Detailed Characteristics*, Series PC(1)-1D to 53D, tables 96 and 129 for each state. In addition, references to furniture employment for 1966 and 1969 are based on the *Annual Survey of Manufactures: Statistics for States, Standard Metropolitan Statistical Areas, and Large Industrial Counties*, for the respective areas and years. Population data for 1970 are from the *U.S. Census of Population, 1970: Distribution of the Negro Population by County*, PC(S1)-1, Table 1, and *General Population Characteristics, United States Summary*, PC(1)-B1, Table 67. In the use of 1960 and 1970 population data, SMSAs and urban statistics will be based on Standard Metropolitan Statistical Areas of 250,000 population or more.

TABLE 25. Furniture Industry
Percent Negro Employment by Job Category
United States Regions, 1964–1970

Region	Total					White Collar					Blue Collar				
	1964	1966	1967	1969	1970	1964	1966	1967	1969	1970	1964	1966	1967	1969	1970
New England	2.6	1.2	2.2	1.1	—	0.3	0.1	1.2	0.3	—	3.4	1.5	2.4	1.3	—
Middle Atlantic	6.1	6.9	8.5	10.4	7.9	1.6	1.7	2.0	3.3	3.3	7.5	8.5	10.1	12.3	9.1
South	6.9	16.2	18.0	19.6	19.5	0.5	0.8	1.1	1.5	1.7	8.1	18.5	20.7	22.6	22.5
Midwest	6.2	7.1	7.0	6.1	6.6	0.5	0.7	1.1	1.1	1.3	8.5	8.9	8.6	7.7	8.4
West (Pacific)	8.1	10.0	9.5	7.8	—	1.1	1.7	2.0	1.3	—	10.1	12.4	11.5	9.5	—
United States	6.4	11.5	12.7	13.4	13.2	0.8	1.0	1.2	1.6	1.7	8.0	13.8	15.1	16.1	15.9

Sources: Tables 22, 28, 29, 33, 38, and 43.

TABLE 26. *Furniture Industry*
Percent Negro Employment by Job Category
Ten Major Employment States, 1966-1970

	Total				White Collar				Blue Collar			
	1966	1967	1969	1970	1966	1967	1969	1970	1966	1967	1969	1970
North Carolina	11.6	13.4	15.1	14.4	0.7	0.7	1.2	1.6	13.1	15.2	17.1	16.4
California	10.0	11.0	9.7	8.9	1.7	2.2	1.5	1.9	12.4	13.5	12.1	10.8
New York	4.0	5.7	7.3	7.7	1.7	1.7	2.9	3.4	4.7	6.9	8.7	9.1
Pennsylvania	5.2	6.2	10.0	6.4	1.0	0.3	2.0	1.7	6.5	7.3	11.7	7.5
Illinois	16.3	16.5	15.6	16.1	1.4	1.8	2.1	2.1	21.7	21.4	22.5	23.4
Virginia	19.0	20.9	23.5	25.2	0.7	0.7	1.0	1.4	22.1	24.2	27.2	28.9
Indiana	1.4	1.7	2.5	1.7	0.1	0.2	0.5	0.3	1.6	2.0	2.9	2.0
Tennessee	15.1	14.1	13.9	14.4	1.3	1.6	1.8	1.9	17.2	16.1	15.9	16.8
Michigan	7.1	5.0	5.7	5.7	0.6	0.5	0.8	1.1	8.9	6.3	7.3	7.3
Ohio	6.7	7.8	6.4	6.6	0.8	2.3	1.3	1.6	9.1	9.7	8.2	8.3
United States	11.5	12.7	13.4	13.2	1.0	1.2	1.6	1.7	13.8	15.1	16.1	15.9

Sources: Appendix Tables A-2 to A-5 and A-29 to A-68.

force as of 1969. This number represented a substantial decline from the mid-1960s figures.

As would be expected, Negro employment has not fared well in the New England industry, the primary limitations being the lack of black residents and the declining industry. In 1960, 2.3 percent of the region's population and 1.6 percent of regional furniture employment was black. By 1970, the region's black population had increased to 3.3 percent, but because of a declining industry, EEOC figures placed the 1969 employment level at only 1.1 percent (Table 28).

An interesting aspect of Negro employment in the New England furniture industry is its heavy concentration in the SMSA areas of 250,000 or more population, although total industry employment is relatively low in those areas. For example, in the New England industry as of 1960, 86 percent of all Negro employment, but only 34 percent of total employment, was in the large SMSAs. This represents the largest variation found in any region. The variation is partially explained by the fact that throughout the 1960s approximately 70 percent of New England's Negro population, but only 50 percent of its total population, resided in the SMSAs of 250,000 or more population.

The percentage of Negro employment in the industry, in both blue collar and white collar jobs, has fluctuated considerably in recent years (Tables 27 and 28). However, since the number of blacks in the New England sector of the industry is so small, these fluctuations in statistics are not necessarily indicative of any major changes. For example, only 88 of the 7,997 employees working in furniture companies employing 100 or more workers in 1969 were Negroes; 83 of these held blue collar jobs, the heaviest concentration being in the laborer category. Of the five blacks in white collar positions, three held clerical jobs, one was a technician, and one was in the management category (see Appendix Table A-9). Given the small black population and the declining industry, Negro employment in the New England furniture industry is not likely to improve in the near future.

MIDDLE ATLANTIC STATES

As of 1969 New York, Pennsylvania, and New Jersey accounted for the third largest block of furniture employment in the United States, or approximately 16.3 percent of the indus-

TABLE 27. *Furniture Industry*
Percent Distribution of Negro Employment by Occupational Group and Region 1966 and 1969

Occupational Group	New England 1966	New England 1969	Middle Atlantic 1966	Middle Atlantic 1969	South 1966	South 1969	Midwest 1966	Midwest 1969	West (Pacific) 1966	West (Pacific) 1969
Officials and managers	—	1.1	0.9	1.1	0.1	0.3	0.5	1.0	1.0	1.3
Professionals	—	—	0.6	0.2	*	*	0.1	0.1	—	0.2
Technicians	—	1.1	0.1	0.4	*	0.1	0.3	0.5	0.6	0.4
Sales workers	2.1	—	—	0.1	*	*	—	0.1	—	0.1
Office and clerical workers	—	3.5	4.3	5.1	0.6	0.6	1.5	2.7	2.3	1.4
Total white collar	2.1	5.7	5.9	6.9	0.7	1.0	2.4	4.4	3.9	3.4
Craftsmen	4.3	17.1	7.9	15.6	9.5	10.1	10.7	14.9	14.4	14.5
Operatives	38.3	26.1	56.6	49.4	40.7	45.1	56.5	43.0	41.1	51.7
Laborers	55.3	50.0	27.6	26.9	45.3	40.5	28.7	35.3	37.6	28.6
Service workers	—	1.1	2.0	1.2	3.8	3.3	1.7	2.4	3.0	1.8
Total blue collar	97.9	94.3	94.1	93.1	99.3	99.0	97.6	95.6	96.1	96.6
Total	100.0	100.0	100.0	100.0	100.0	100.0	100.0	100.0	100.0	100.0

Sources: Computed from Appendix Tables A-7, A-9, A-11, A-13, A-16, A-18, A-21, A-23, A-26, and A-28.

* Less than 0.05 percent.

TABLE 28. *Furniture Industry*
Percent Negro Employment by Sex and Occupational Group
New England, 1964-1969

Occupational Group	All Employees				Male				Female			
	1964	1966	1967	1969	1964	1966	1967	1969	1964	1966	1967	1969
Officials and managers	—	—	0.5	0.2	—	—	0.5	0.2	—	—	—	—
Professionals	—	—	—	—	—	—	—	—	—	—	—	—
Technicians	—	—	—	1.0	—	—	—	1.1	—	—	—	—
Service workers	—	0.8	—	—	—	0.8	—	—	—	—	—	—
Office and clerical workers	0.7	—	2.5	0.5	1.8	—	—	—	—	—	3.0	0.6
Total white collar	0.3	0.1	1.2	0.3	0.4	0.2	0.3	0.2	—	—	2.7	0.5
Craftsmen	1.4	0.4	2.3	0.9	1.4	0.5	2.4	1.0	—	—	1.4	0.6
Operatives	4.8	1.1	2.2	0.9	4.3	1.2	2.0	0.7	7.7	0.5	2.8	1.4
Laborers	4.1	3.0	2.8	2.0	4.3	3.3	2.9	1.6	—	2.4	2.5	3.1
Service workers	—	—	7.1	0.8	—	—	7.1	—	—	—	—	7.7
Total blue collar	3.4	1.5	2.4	1.3	3.1	1.6	2.4	1.0	5.9	1.3	2.5	2.1
Total	2.6	1.2	2.2	1.1	2.6	1.3	2.1	0.9	2.7	0.8	2.6	1.6

Sources: Appendix Tables A-6 to A-9.

try's employment. Although this represents an appreciable decline from the level of 23.7 percent shown by the 1960 Census, the total number of employees has stabilized somewhat in recent years.

Because of a relatively high percentage of Negro residents, the Middle Atlantic region has been among the leading regions in terms of Negro employment in furniture manufacturing. In both 1960 and 1970 this region had the highest percentage of Negro residents of any region outside the South: 8.1 percent and 10.6 percent, respectively. As a result, the level of black employment in the industry in 1969, according to EEOC data, was 10.4 percent, or almost three percentage points higher than all other nonsouthern regions.

Unlike the New England furniture industry, the industry in the Middle Atlantic region is concentrated in SMSA areas. This works to the advantage of Negroes seeking employment, for, as of 1960, 93.0 percent of all Negroes in the region were located in SMSAs of 250,000 or more population. Consequently, 96.3 percent of all Negro employment in the furniture industry was located in these areas. By 1970 the Negro population concentration in large SMSAs had increased to 94.2 percent, no doubt further increasing the concentration of Negro employment in furniture. Because of this population concentration, very few Negroes are found in nonurban furniture centers.

In the latter part of the 1960s, as the economy expanded, Negroes made quite impressive gains in the Middle Atlantic furniture industry. From 1966 to 1969 every blue collar category except service workers, and every white collar category, experienced a constant increase in the percentage of blacks employed (Table 29). The Middle Atlantic region has done quite well in the area of upgrading and hiring blacks for white collar positions. In fact, since 1966 the performance of companies there has equaled or surpassed all other regions. However, most of the white collar jobs are of a clerical nature (Table 27).

For furniture employees in the Middle Atlantic region, and particularly for Negro blue collar workers, 1970 was a poor year. The effect of a declining economy is particularly evident among Negro blue collar workers, as every category except service workers declined in number. The net result was for the total percentage of Negro employment to decline from a high of 10.4 percent in 1969 to 7.9 percent in 1970. If it had not been for the industry's ability to retain most of those Ne-

TABLE 29. *Furniture Industry*
Percent Negro Employment by Sex and Occupational Group
Middle Atlantic States, 1964-1970

Occupational Group	All Employees					Male					Female				
	1964	1966	1967	1969	1970	1964	1966	1967	1969	1970	1964	1966	1967	1969	1970
Officials and managers	0.5	0.9	1.0	1.7	1.9	0.5	0.9	0.9	1.6	1.8	—	1.5	1.4	4.9	3.9
Professionals	1.1	1.1	1.5	1.7	1.7	1.2	1.1	1.7	1.2	1.5	—	—	—	8.0	2.9
Technicians	—	0.9	1.2	2.1	2.9	—	0.9	1.2	2.2	3.1	—	—	—	2.0	—
Sales workers	—	—	0.1	0.4	0.5	—	—	0.1	0.2	0.3	—	—	—	2.2	2.9
Office and clerical workers	2.9	2.9	3.4	5.8	5.7	2.9	3.3	4.7	6.0	5.0	2.8	2.7	2.9	5.7	6.0
Total white collar	1.6	1.7	2.0	3.3	3.3	1.0	1.3	1.6	2.1	2.1	2.7	2.6	2.7	5.5	5.6
Craftsmen	5.6	3.4	4.2	9.2	6.3	5.0	3.2	3.8	9.1	6.3	11.9	6.3	9.1	10.9	6.8
Operatives	8.4	9.1	10.8	12.8	9.0	7.8	9.4	11.2	12.1	9.7	11.9	7.8	9.0	15.3	6.5
Laborers	6.8	12.1	14.0	14.8	11.6	8.7	11.9	15.5	17.1	12.2	0.3	12.8	7.3	6.4	9.9
Service workers	12.2	8.7	7.8	7.1	11.2	11.3	8.6	8.1	7.2	11.7	21.4	9.5	2.8	5.9	4.9
Total blue collar	7.5	8.5	10.1	12.3	9.1	7.4	8.4	10.4	12.4	9.6	8.2	9.1	8.5	12.1	7.6
Total	6.1	6.9	8.5	10.4	7.9	6.2	7.0	9.0	10.5	8.2	5.8	6.5	6.5	9.9	7.0

Sources: Appendix Tables A-10 to A-14.

groes already in white collar positions, the percentage of Negro employment in this industry would have dropped to the lowest point since the early 1960s.

The national trend of women replacing men in the furniture industry may be developing belatedly in the Middle Atlantic region. Although it is too early to say with certainty, the 1970 data indicate that this may be occurring. From 1969 to 1970, as total male employment for companies employing 100 or more workers declined, total female employment reached a new high. Negro women, however, did not share in the gain (Appendix Tables A-13 to A-14).

New York

Having once been the dominant state in furniture manufacturing, New York dropped from second to third place in terms of total employment during the 1960s. In spite of a drop in rank, as of 1969 the state employed approximately 36,200 furniture workers.

The large number of furniture jobs, when combined with a 1970 Negro population of 11.9 percent and an urban concentration of the industry, has been advantageous for the Negro. Particularly in New York City, furniture manufacturing has been a sizable source of Negro employment. Since the New York City SMSA accounts for more than half of the state's total furniture employment and is also the residence of 87.0 percent of the state's 1970 total Negro population (16.3 percent of the New York City SMSA's 1970 population), almost all Negro furniture workers are located in the one SMSA. In contrast, a furniture center like Jamestown reports virtually no Negro employment.

Throughout the 1960s the level of Negro employment in New York did not seem to increase very much. The 1960 Census reported the level at 7.0 percent, and by 1970 the EEOC data indicated a level of only 7.7 percent. An examination of Table 30 indicates that a contrasting of 1960 and 1970 may be misleading in that the 7.7 percent has come about after a series of increases since at least 1966, when the level was estimated to be 4.0 percent. Such a variation is possibly attributable to shortcomings in the EEOC data. Much of the variation, however, is probably explained by what appears to have been a decline in the state's industry employment in the early 1960s

TABLE 30. *Furniture Industry*
Percent Negro Employment by Sex and Occupational Group
New York, 1966-1970

Occupational Group	All Employees				Male				Female			
	1966	1967	1969	1970	1966	1967	1969	1970	1966	1967	1969	1970
Officials and managers	0.8	0.8	1.4	2.0	0.9	0.9	1.2	1.8	—	—	4.5	4.1
Professionals	1.0	1.9	2.0	1.6	1.1	2.2	1.5	1.8	—	—	8.3	—
Technicians	1.1	1.9	2.4	2.4	1.2	2.0	2.2	2.6	—	—	4.3	—
Service workers	—	—	—	0.2	—	—	—	—	—	—	—	4.0
Office and clerical workers	2.9	2.7	5.5	6.1	4.2	3.9	3.8	5.0	2.5	2.3	6.1	6.4
Total white collar	1.7	1.7	2.9	3.4	1.3	1.4	1.3	2.0	2.3	2.1	5.8	6.0
Craftsmen	2.1	2.5	4.8	6.9	1.9	2.2	4.9	6.6	3.8	6.1	3.9	8.6
Operatives	3.0	5.7	7.7	7.1	2.9	5.9	8.0	8.1	3.3	4.7	6.5	3.4
Laborers	13.2	13.9	13.5	15.0	14.3	15.0	16.3	14.0	6.3	8.8	5.8	17.4
Service workers	8.4	7.2	13.3	12.2	7.9	8.0	13.0	13.1	15.0	—	15.8	4.8
Total blue collar	4.7	6.9	8.7	9.1	4.8	7.1	9.4	9.2	4.1	5.9	6.0	8.7
Total	4.0	5.7	7.3	7.7	4.2	6.0	7.7	7.7	3.3	4.4	5.9	7.8

Sources: Appendix Tables A-37 to A-40.

and a resurgence since the mid-1960s. As reported above, the 1960 and 1969 employment totals were 37,900 and 36,200, respectively. In 1966, however, the level was estimated to be only 33,100. Thus, Negroes could have been affected more severely than other employees by layoffs in the early part of the decade, but if so, they have regained lost ground since 1966.

Pennsylvania

Although furniture industry employment continues to grow in Pennsylvania, increasing from 22,200 in 1960 to 28,700 in 1969, it has not been a sizable source of employment for Negroes. The only real exception has been Philadelphia. Although in 1960 the Philadelphia SMSA employed only 29.3 percent of the state's furniture workers, it accounted for 93.7 percent of the state's Negro employment in furniture, being the home of 78.9 percent of the state's Negro population. By 1970, the SMSA's black population had increased to 17.5 percent from 15.4 percent in 1960, and consequently accounted for 83.1 percent of the state's black population. Therefore, as in New York, few Negroes in Pennsylvania are to be found in furniture plants outside the largest metropolitan area.

The percentage of Negroes in the state's industry changed very little in the early 1960s. Whereas in 1960 the level was 5.9 percent, by 1966 EEOC data showed a level of approximately 5.2 percent (Table 31). During the years of economic expansion, particularly from 1966 to 1969, black employment increased fairly substantially. The increase was most noticeable in blue collar jobs, but some improvement did occur in white collar jobs, principally in those of a clerical nature. Unfortunately, 1970 brought setbacks for Negroes. With the deteriorating economic conditions, total Negro employment among firms employing 100 or more workers declined from 10.0 percent to a level only slightly above the 1960 figure of 5.9 percent. Thus, among the top ten furniture states (see Table 26), Pennsylvania ranked eighth in terms of the level of Negro employment as of 1970.

SOUTH

The South actually consists of three regions: the South Atlantic, the East South Central and the West South Central, with the South Atlantic being by far the region of greatest

TABLE 31. *Furniture Industry*
Percent Negro Employment by Sex and Occupational Group
Pennsylvania, 1966-1970

Occupational Group	All Employees				Male				Female			
	1966	1967	1969	1970	1966	1967	1969	1970	1966	1967	1969	1970
Officials and managers	0.5	—	1.3	1.2	0.5	—	1.3	1.1	—	—	2.7	2.6
Professionals	1.2	—	0.8	1.4	1.2	—	0.8	0.7	—	—	—	14.3
Technicians	0.6	—	0.8	3.0	0.7	—	0.9	3.2	—	—	—	—
Sales workers	—	—	0.4	—	—	—	0.5	—	—	—	—	—
Office and clerical workers	1.4	0.7	3.2	2.4	2.3	1.6	5.9	2.0	0.8	0.3	2.0	2.6
Total white collar	1.0	0.3	2.0	1.7	1.0	0.3	2.1	1.3	0.7	0.3	1.9	2.5
Craftsmen	2.0	1.1	8.5	2.9	2.1	1.1	8.8	2.7	—	—	3.9	5.0
Operatives	8.1	9.1	12.4	8.4	8.5	10.5	11.2	9.6	6.5	2.3	17.5	5.1
Laborers	6.3	9.0	14.6	9.1	7.0	10.1	17.3	10.8	3.9	5.0	2.4	3.6
Service workers	6.5	2.2	1.4	7.5	6.6	2.3	1.5	7.6	5.6	—	—	5.3
Total blue collar	6.5	7.3	11.7	7.5	6.7	8.1	11.7	8.3	5.2	3.1	12.0	4.7
Total	5.2	6.2	10.0	6.4	5.5	7.0	10.2	7.1	3.8	2.3	8.8	4.2

Sources: Appendix Tables A-41 to A-44.

furniture employment. For analytic purposes the three regions will be considered as one. This one region accounted for 42.3 percent of all U. S. furniture employment in 1969. Although most other regions experienced a decline in standing during the decade, the South increased its share of total employment by more than five percentage points.

Lower wage rates, an abundance of lumber, and major furniture markets in High Point, North Carolina and Atlanta, Georgia are factors in the continued movement to the South that began in the last century. Because of a very tight labor market in some furniture centers in Virginia and North Carolina, this movement, if it continues, will probably shift westward, to such states as Mississippi, Arkansas, and Texas. Recent growth in furniture employment in these states suggests that such a trend is already taking place.

Southern Negroes made considerable gains in furniture industry employment in the 1960s. Since Negroes made up 19.1 percent of the South's population in 1970, it is not too surprising that a relatively large percentage of Negroes occupy furniture-manufacturing jobs. Whereas 11.8 percent of the southern furniture work force in 1960 was made up of Negroes, the succeeding decade saw the percentage for employers of 100 workers or more climb to a high of 19.6 percent in 1969.

The level of black employment in the South varies significantly from state to state (Table 32). From highs in 1970 of 54.2 percent, 34.4 percent, 34.4 percent, and 30.8 percent in South Carolina, Georgia, Mississippi, and Alabama respectively, the level drops to as low as 4.5 percent in Kentucky. As in other regions, it appears that the availability of Negro labor is a major factor in the variation. For example, using the 1970 census, the states listed above are four of the top five states in terms of the percentage of Negro residents, reporting 30.5, 25.9, 36.8 and 26.2 percent, respectively. In contrast, Kentucky reported a level of only 7.2 percent.

As might be expected, the states with the very high levels of Negro employment tend to be the leading states in terms of Negro white collar employment. This is primarily because the majority of Negro white collar employees in these states are in positions (managers and male clericals) that are often filled from internal labor sources. Since Negroes make up such a large source of internal labor, only blatant discrimination would be likely to prevent a relatively large percentage of Negro white

TABLE 32. *Furniture Industry*
Percent Negro Employment by State and Job Category
South, 1966-1970

State [a]	Total				White Collar				Blue Collar			
	1966	1967	1969	1970	1966	1967	1969	1970	1966	1967	1969	1970
Alabama	19.4	23.6	30.9	30.8	1.0	0.4	0.4	1.2	23.4	27.3	34.8	34.9
Arkansas	11.3	8.8	4.2	11.2	0.3	0.3	0.1	0.6	12.9	10.0	5.0	12.9
Florida	13.3	15.7	17.4	17.5	0.6	2.5	1.0	1.6	15.5	18.0	20.1	20.6
Georgia	26.7	25.8	28.8	34.4	0.7	1.0	0.9	2.3	30.4	29.9	35.1	39.2
Kentucky	3.2	4.7	3.1	4.5	0.3	0.7	0.5	0.7	3.7	5.4	3.6	5.1
Mississippi	34.0	37.8	40.3	34.4	2.3	2.7	4.1	2.7	39.3	43.5	46.4	40.6
North Carolina	11.6	13.4	15.1	14.4	0.7	0.7	1.2	1.6	13.1	15.2	17.1	16.4
South Carolina	47.7	40.3	53.8	54.2	1.2	0.8	1.5	3.1	51.8	46.3	60.7	62.6
Tennessee	15.1	14.1	13.9	14.4	1.3	1.6	1.8	1.9	17.2	16.1	15.9	16.8
Texas	9.1	11.7	17.0	16.4	0.3	1.1	1.8	1.2	10.9	13.8	20.2	19.7
Virginia	19.0	20.9	23.5	25.2	0.7	0.7	1.0	1.4	22.1	24.2	27.2	28.9

Sources: 1966: U.S. Equal Employment Opportunity Commission, *Job Patterns for Minorities and Women in Private Industry, 1966,* Report No. 1 (Washington: The Commission, 1968), Part II.
1967: U.S. Equal Employment Opportunity Commission, *Job Patterns for Minorities and Women in Private Industry, 1967,* Report No. 2 (Washington: The Commission, 1970), Vol. I.
1969: U.S. Equal Employment Opportunity Commission.
1970: U.S. Equal Employment Opportunity Commission.

[a] Louisiana, Maryland, and Oklahoma have been eliminated due to the small number of reporting units.

collar employment. In 1970 Mississippi, Georgia, and South Carolina reported that over 2 percent of their white collar employees were Negroes. Although these levels are high by intraregional and even by most interregional comparisons, they nevertheless are quite low in comparison to the overall level of black employment in the South and in these states. The South reports a considerably lower distribution of blacks in white collar jobs than any other region (Table 27).

In spite of the South's relatively poor showing in Negro white collar employment, slow but steady progress has occurred in every white collar category since 1964 (Table 33). Interviews with southern industry representatives have indicated that some companies are aware of underutilization of Negroes in white collar positions and are actively seeking to correct the situation. In addition, it should be recognized that in an absolute sense the South, by virtue of its large number of blacks and large number of furniture jobs, accounts for a major portion of the industry's total Negro white collar force. As of 1970, 328 of the nation's total of 874 Negro white collar employees were in the South.

The South has for a number of years employed a large number of blacks in blue collar jobs. In fact, since the mid-1960s the percentage of blacks in the furniture industry has exceeded the percentage of blacks in the region's total population. A closer examination of blue collar positions shows that the Negro has made substantial gains in the higher-ranking categories while maintaining a relatively stable level in the laborer category. Only in the service jobs has there been a decline.

The South, in contrast to other regions, does not have a high concentration of Negroes living in the region's SMSAs of 250,-000 or more population. As of 1960 only 32.5 percent of the South's population, and only 30.4 percent of its Negro population lived in such areas. By 1970 both percentages had increased to 40.6 percent. Since the vast majority of the southern industry is located outside these SMSAs, there is a considerable degree of overlapping of Negro population concentrations and furniture employment. Should the rapid migration of southern blacks to the large urban centers continue, employment opportunities for blacks will be seriously reduced. Because there are currently some nonurban areas in the South with low Negro concentrations and others with high Negro concentrations, it is

TABLE 33. Furniture Industry
Percent Negro Employment by Sex and Occupational Group
South, 1964-1970

Occupational Group	All Employees					Male					Female				
	1964	1966	1967	1969	1970	1964	1966	1967	1969	1970	1964	1966	1967	1969	1970
Officials and managers	0.3	0.4	0.6	1.2	1.4	0.3	0.4	0.6	1.2	1.4	—	0.5	0.5	1.5	1.1
Professionals	—	0.1	0.2	0.3	0.4	—	0.1	0.1	0.2	0.3	—	—	1.5	1.0	1.2
Technicians	—	0.1	1.3	1.4	1.6	—	0.1	1.4	1.4	1.4	—	—	—	0.8	3.6
Sales workers	—	0.1	0.1	0.3	0.3	—	0.1	0.1	0.2	0.2	—	—	—	1.6	1.6
Office and clerical workers	1.0	1.5	1.8	2.2	2.5	2.9	4.2	5.1	5.7	6.8	0.3	0.6	0.6	1.2	1.3
Total white collar	0.5	0.8	1.1	1.5	1.7	0.5	1.0	1.3	1.6	1.8	0.3	0.6	0.6	1.2	1.3
Craftsmen	2.8	7.6	8.0	10.3	10.5	3.0	7.9	8.3	10.2	10.2	—	5.2	5.7	10.9	12.2
Operatives	11.8	16.6	19.1	22.6	23.0	12.5	16.6	19.1	22.3	22.3	6.0	17.1	19.0	23.4	24.9
Laborers	5.8	28.8	31.5	30.6	31.1	6.3	29.5	30.9	31.7	32.6	2.8	26.1	33.3	28.4	28.7
Service workers	30.9	39.7	37.3	38.2	33.0	29.0	38.5	36.2	35.6	31.4	72.7	52.7	51.2	60.8	45.9
Total blue collar	8.1	18.5	20.7	22.6	22.5	8.5	18.4	19.9	22.0	21.6	4.3	19.2	23.7	24.4	25.0
Total	6.9	16.2	18.0	19.6	19.5	7.6	16.6	17.8	19.5	19.0	3.0	14.5	18.9	20.1	20.8

Sources: Appendix Tables A-15 to A-19.

important to consider local population characteristics before drawing conclusions concerning employment opportunities in a state or region. For example, although the percentage of Arkansas' black population is almost twice the percentage of Negro furniture employment in the state as reported by the EEOC survey, the variation is primarily the result of a mismatching of areas of high Negro population concentrations and furniture employment. A major portion of the industry is located in Fort Smith, where, as of 1970, only 4.2 percent of the population was black.

In some southern plants employing rather large numbers of Negro workers there has been some apprehension over the increasing level of Negro employment. In one large plant where Negro employment is approaching 40 percent, a level almost twice that of the community's black population, there was the feeling that such a large element of Negro labor might make the company more vulnerable to union organizing efforts.[150] As discussed earlier, this opinion is not limited to the South. Not only are some companies apprehensive about potential union gains caused by the increasing employment of blacks, but there is also concern that after a plant reaches a certain level of Negro employment the number of applications from the white population will decline drastically, ultimately creating a totally black work force. This has happened not only in some furniture plants but also in other industries, regardless of the regional location of the plants.[151]

The trend toward replacing male labor with female labor is particularly prevalent in the South. Between 1967 and 1970 the number of men reported in the EEOC survey dropped by almost 11,000, while the number of women increased by almost 7,000 (Appendix Tables A-17 to A-19). For Negro men the decline occurred from only 1969 to 1970, reflecting at least in part the general economic conditions. As Negro men were declining in number, the numbers of Negro women continued to increase. It remains to be seen if the decline in Negro male workers will continue when the economy picks up, but there can be little doubt that the current trend in the South is for higher employment levels for female labor, and particularly for Negro women.

---

150. Interview, January 1972.

151. Herbert R. Northrup, "The Negro in the Automobile Industry," *Basic Industry, op. cit.,* pp. 105-106.

North Carolina

North Carolina is without question the furniture center of the nation and its percentage of national employment in the industry continues to increase constantly. In 1960, North Carolina had 43,900 furniture workers, or 11.7 percent of total national employment in the industry. Total employment has increased substantially since then, to a total of 63,000 employees, or 13.8 percent of total employment, in 1969. Aided not only by traditionally lower wage rates in the South but also by the national market at High Point, the existing furniture industry has expanded considerably in recent years and additional companies have been attracted to the state.

Since Negroes make up approximately 22.2 percent of the state's population, North Carolina has the largest number of Negro employees in furniture manufacturing of any state. The relative percentages, however, are not as large as might be expected. For example, in 1960 Negro employment in the state's industry was estimated at only 8.7 percent of total employment. The level for employers of 100 or more workers was up to 11.6 percent in 1966 and 14.4 percent in 1970 (Table 34). Locational considerations have a direct bearing on these relatively low percentages. The counties with the largest Negro populations are generally located in the eastern portion of the state, and the more urban areas of the central part of the state also have quite high levels of Negro population. The furniture industry, on the other hand, is concentrated in the nonurban areas of the central region and in the western counties of the state. In the few counties where there is an overlapping of Negro and furniture industry concentration, such as High Point's Guilford County, it is not unusual for major companies to employ a proportion of Negroes considerably higher than that of the area's total population.[152]

North Carolina, like many other furniture states, reports a wide discrepancy between the level of Negroes employed in blue collar jobs and the level of Negroes employed in white collar jobs. Until the economic downturn in 1970, Negro blue collar workers had increased to a high of 17.1 percent of all blue collar employment (Table 34). Such an increase occurred in all categories except the lowest, indicating an upgrading of blacks. In 1970, Negroes managed to retain most of their blue

---

152. Interview, January 1972.

TABLE 34. *Furniture Industry*

Percent Negro Employment by Sex and Occupational Group
North Carolina, 1966-1970

Occupational Group	All Employees				Male				Female			
	1966	1967	1969	1970	1966	1967	1969	1970	1966	1967	1969	1970
Officials and managers	0.4	0.3	0.8	1.0	0.4	0.2	0.7	1.0	0.9	0.9	1.7	—
Professionals	—	—	—	—	—	—	—	—	—	—	—	—
Technicians	—	0.3	1.0	0.6	—	0.3	1.2	0.7	—	—	—	—
Sales workers	0.1	0.2	0.5	0.2	0.2	0.2	0.3	—	—	—	7.7	2.0
Office and clerical workers	1.3	1.3	2.0	3.1	3.1	3.7	3.9	9.6	0.7	0.5	1.4	1.4
Total white collar	0.7	0.7	1.2	1.6	0.7	0.7	1.1	1.8	0.7	0.5	1.4	1.3
Craftsmen	5.5	6.4	7.4	8.1	5.8	6.5	7.0	7.6	3.0	5.6	9.7	10.4
Operatives	13.6	16.0	18.4	17.6	13.3	14.9	16.7	16.2	15.3	20.7	24.3	21.4
Laborers	18.9	22.5	25.1	24.9	17.8	20.3	23.4	22.7	23.4	28.7	28.3	28.3
Service workers	37.6	34.2	33.4	30.2	36.0	33.4	30.1	28.9	56.9	45.2	56.6	38.6
Total blue collar	13.1	15.2	17.1	16.4	12.6	13.9	15.2	14.6	15.8	21.0	23.2	21.6
Total	11.6	13.4	15.1	14.4	11.5	12.6	13.7	13.0	12.2	16.9	19.3	18.2

Sources: Appendix Tables A-29 to A-32.

collar progress by declining only slightly in most categories and actually increasing in the craftsmen category. Although black employment in the white collar area stood at only 1.6 percent as of 1970, the level has increased gradually since 1966. In spite of the economic conditions in 1970, the white collar category increased from 1.2 to 1.6 percent from 1969 to 1970, with the areas of managers and clericals accounting for almost the entire increase.

The national trend of replacing men with women in the furniture work force is particularly evident in North Carolina. Whereas in 1966 women made up 16.9 percent of total employment in the industry, by 1970 the figure was 27.2 percent. Negro women have increased from 2.1 percent to 5.0 percent of the total furniture work force. The decline in men is occurring in virtually every category. Only in 1971 did the number of Negro men decline, but the number of Negro women has consistently increased.

Virginia

Virginia is second only to North Carolina in the increase of total furniture industry employment in the past decade. By increasing employment from 16,900 in 1960 to 25,900 in 1969, the state has moved from ninth place to sixth place in terms of total furniture industry employment. In addition, if growth continues at anywhere near the current rate, Virginia could easily rank fourth by the end of this decade.

Because Virginia has an expanding industry and a state population that is 18.5 percent black, ample employment opportunities have existed for Negroes. According to EEOC data, 14.5 percent of the total furniture work force in 1960 was Negro; by 1966 the figure had risen to 19.0 percent. As Table 35 shows, in the years since 1966 the percentage constantly increased until in 1970 the level was 25.2 percent—a level that far exceeds all other leading states.

The impressive total figures for Negro employment do not carry over to all job categories. Although there has been gradual improvement in almost all blue collar categories in recent years, particularly in the operative area, white collar categories have not improved at such an impressive rate. In spite of some gradual improvement in the white collar area in recent years, as of 1969 and 1970 only two other top ten states had lower percentages of Negroes in white collar jobs (Table 26).

TABLE 35. *Furniture Industry*
Percent Negro Employment by Sex and Occupational Group
Virginia, 1966-1970

Occupational Group	All Employees				Male				Female			
	1966	1967	1969	1970	1966	1967	1969	1970	1966	1967	1969	1970
Officials and managers	0.3	0.5	0.7	1.3	0.3	0.5	0.7	1.3	—	—	—	—
Professionals	—	—	1.0	0.9	—	—	1.2	0.9	—	—	—	—
Technicians	0.5	—	1.6	1.8	0.5	—	1.8	1.3	—	—	—	10.0
Sales workers	—	0.5	—	—	—	0.5	—	—	—	—	—	—
Office and clerical workers	1.3	1.2	1.5	1.8	3.7	3.0	4.5	2.7	0.5	0.7	0.9	1.6
Total white collar	0.7	0.7	1.0	1.4	0.8	0.8	1.1	1.3	0.5	0.6	0.9	1.7
Craftsmen	10.9	12.2	14.7	13.5	11.3	12.5	14.0	12.9	2.5	6.4	26.5	21.5
Operatives	14.1	17.9	26.1	30.4	14.7	18.9	26.0	30.0	9.5	13.4	26.2	31.5
Laborers	38.8	37.8	38.5	40.1	36.4	35.6	34.0	37.5	47.7	44.0	46.6	44.1
Service workers	43.5	50.9	36.4	36.1	42.1	49.3	32.4	33.2	68.8	70.8	81.8	81.3
Total blue collar	22.1	24.2	27.2	28.9	20.9	22.9	24.3	26.1	29.9	29.7	37.0	37.2
Total	19.0	20.9	23.5	25.2	18.7	20.4	21.4	23.1	20.7	22.7	29.9	30.9

Sources: Appendix Tables A-49 to A-52.

As in some of the other states considered, there appears to be an exodus of male labor in both blue collar and white collar positions. There has been a slight decline in the number of Negro men since 1967, although both the number and percentage of Negro white collar employees has increased. In addition, most of the women entering the industry in recent years have been black. For example, between 1967 and 1970 the total number of women increased by 952; 660 of them were Negroes (see Appendix Tables A-50 to A-52).

Total Negro employment in Virginia has not been adversely affected by a mismatching of areas of Negro population concentration and furniture employment. The majority of Negroes are located in the non-SMSA areas, where furniture employment is also found. Furniture manufacturing is heavily concentrated in the southwestern portion of the state, particularly in Henry County where such cities as Bassett, Stanley, and Martinsville are located. Although the 1960 population of Henry County was approximately 22.6 percent Negro, it is not unusual for some of the major plants in this area to have a percentage of Negro employment that is considerably in excess of that for the total population.[153]

Tennessee

Tennessee continues to be a growth state in terms of furniture employment. Whereas in 1960 there were 14,500 furniture employees in the state, by 1969 there were 22,300. This growth, when combined with a Negro population of 15.8 percent, has increased the Negro's employment opportunities.

Employment opportunities for the Negro were quite good in the early 1960s but have remained relatively stable since the middle of the decade. Whereas the level of Negro employment in 1960 was 11.0 percent, by 1966 the EEOC survey was indicating a level of 15.1 percent. Since 1966 the level has fluctuated between 13.9 and 15.1 percent (Table 36). In spite of the quite constant level since the middle of the decade, the numbers of both blue collar and white collar jobs held by blacks have increased each year. Although there have been fluctuations within the categories, major increases have occurred in the categories of craftsmen and operatives. In addition, some improve-

---

153. Interview, January 1972.

TABLE 36. *Furniture Industry*
Percent Negro Employment by Sex and Occupational Group
Tennessee, 1966-1970

Occupational Group	All Employees				Male				Female			
	1966	1967	1969	1970	1966	1967	1969	1970	1966	1967	1969	1970
Officials and managers	1.0	0.9	1.4	0.9	1.0	0.9	1.4	0.9	—	—	—	—
Professionals	—	0.8	1.2	1.8	—	—	0.7	1.3	—	10.0	5.3	5.6
Technicians	—	1.3	1.7	2.0	—	1.6	1.8	2.1	—	—	—	—
Sales workers	—	—	—	—	—	—	—	—	—	—	—	—
Office and clerical workers	2.4	3.0	3.0	3.6	5.2	8.1	5.3	7.3	1.3	0.9	1.9	2.1
Total white collar	1.3	1.6	1.8	1.9	1.4	1.8	1.8	1.8	1.2	1.0	2.0	2.1
Craftsmen	3.3	5.1	7.7	6.0	2.9	4.8	6.6	5.3	6.3	9.9	34.0	13.3
Operatives	15.8	16.3	15.1	16.2	12.3	12.5	11.7	13.1	34.2	28.2	26.1	24.7
Laborers	23.7	20.4	18.8	22.4	22.4	19.8	19.9	23.3	28.8	22.1	17.1	21.0
Service workers	34.7	22.4	25.9	23.6	34.7	22.2	24.7	22.9	34.4	25.0	40.0	30.0
Total blue collar	17.2	16.1	15.9	16.8	14.7	13.4	13.7	14.5	29.6	25.7	22.0	22.7
Total	15.1	14.1	13.9	14.4	13.3	12.0	12.0	12.5	23.2	21.4	19.0	19.3

Sources: Appendix Tables A-57 to A-60.

ment has occurred in white collar jobs, with the principal increases occurring in the clerical category. In fact, almost all Negro women in white collar positions held clerical jobs. In general, although the level of Negro blue collar employment has tended to stabilize in recent years, slow but steady improvement has occurred among the white collar positions.

In contrast to other southern furniture states, the Negro population of Tennessee is concentrated in the large SMSA areas (74.3 percent in 1970). Since almost two-thirds of the state's furniture employment is located outside these areas, this restricts the supply of Negro labor available to the industry. The success of Negroes in finding employment in the state's SMSAs has varied significantly. For example, in 1960, Memphis, the dominant SMSA in terms of furniture employment, reported its Negro population and Negro employment in the industry as being 36.2 percent and 51.0 percent, respectively. Memphis alone accounted for 82 percent of the total Negro furniture employment in the state although accounting for only 18 percent of total industry employment. By 1970 Memphis' black population had increased to 37.5 percent, although in most other areas of the state black population levels had declined. Since in recent years the industry has become increasingly concentrated in the northeastern portion of the state, particularly in the Morristown area where relatively few Negroes live, the state's level of Negro employment has not increased appreciably in spite of the interest that area companies have in hiring more Negroes.[154]

Texas, Mississippi, Arkansas, and Georgia

If the percentage of Negro employment in the furniture industry in the South is to increase to much higher levels in the near future, it appears likely that it will have to be as a result of industry expansion into other southern states. Since some of the furniture centers of North Carolina, Virginia, and Tennessee are already experiencing tight labor markets, some with unemployment rates near the 1 percent level, it seems doubtful that any dramatic increases in Negro representation are likely to occur there in the near future. If furniture expansion continues to occur in other southern states, particularly in those with large Negro populations, the regional as well as national

---

154. Interview, March 1972.

percentages of Negro employment may continue to increase for some time. As of 1969, the eleventh, twelfth, thirteenth, and fourteenth ranking states in terms of furniture employment were southern states. Mississippi and Georgia reported total percentages of Negro employment considerably in excess of any of the top ten states (Table 37). Arkansas and Texas reported rather substantial levels of Negro employment, although, as was discussed earlier, the intrastate location of the industry in Arkansas does not match the concentration of the Negro population in the state.

MIDWEST

The Midwest is an area which is frequently divided into two separate regions, the East North Central and West North Central. Because the level of Negro furniture employment is quite similar in these two areas and in order to simplify analysis, they will be discussed as one region. One distinction should be noted, however: the East North Central is by far the major region in terms of furniture employment, employing approximately 85 percent of all midwestern furniture workers.

Although the Midwest, like most nonsouthern areas, has declined in relative standing, it accounts for the second largest block of total furniture employment and Negro furniture employment in the United States. In 1969 the region employed 117,600 workers, or 25.8 percent of total national employment in the industry. In 1960 Negroes made up 4.8 percent of regional employment although Negroes comprise 6.6 percent of the region's population. By 1970 Negro employment in firms employing 100 or more workers had increased to 6.6 percent, although the population level had increased to 8.1 percent.

The 1970 employment level represented very little change since the mid-1960s (Table 38). However, the white collar sector did show a gradual increase in the level of Negro employment in the latter 1960s. Almost all white collar gains for Negro men occurred in the officials and managers category whereas gains for Negro women were almost exclusively in the office and clerical positions (Appendix Tables A-20 to A-24).

An expansion of Tables 39-42 reveals that there are significant variations in the employment of Negroes among the major furniture-manufacturing states of the Midwest. In 1970 Illinois led all midwestern states in both blue collar and white collar em-

TABLE 37. *Furniture Industry*
Percent Negro Employment by Job Category and Sex
Texas, Mississippi, Arkansas, and Georgia, 1966-1970

	Total				White Collar				Blue Collar			
	1966	1967	1969	1970	1966	1967	1969	1970	1966	1967	1969	1970
Texas												
All Employees	9.1	11.7	17.0	16.4	0.3	1.1	1.8	1.2	10.9	13.8	20.2	19.7
Male Employees	10.5	12.5	17.6	16.2	0.4	1.6	2.1	1.3	12.2	14.3	20.6	19.1
Female Employees	4.7	9.6	15.7	17.0	—	—	1.4	1.0	6.2	12.2	19.2	21.2
Mississippi												
All Employees	34.0	37.8	40.3	34.4	2.3	2.7	4.1	2.7	39.3	43.5	46.4	40.6
Male Employees	37.6	40.2	43.0	37.6	3.2	3.8	5.7	3.5	41.9	45.1	48.5	43.2
Female Employees	14.4	28.4	30.8	23.4	0.7	0.4	0.6	1.0	20.5	36.6	38.3	30.4
Arkansas												
All Employees	11.3	8.8	4.2	11.2	0.3	0.3	0.1	0.6	12.9	10.0	5.0	12.9
Male Employees	10.3	8.5	4.3	10.3	0.2	0.4	0.2	0.9	11.5	9.5	5.0	11.8
Female Employees	15.0	9.8	4.0	13.3	0.4	—	—	—	18.8	11.7	4.9	15.7
Georgia												
All Employees	26.7	25.8	28.8	34.4	0.7	1.0	0.9	2.3	30.4	29.9	35.1	39.2
Male Employees	28.6	30.2	33.3	34.0	0.9	1.0	0.9	1.9	31.7	34.0	40.1	39.0
Female Employees	20.1	14.9	20.1	35.0	0.3	1.0	1.1	2.8	25.1	18.0	24.9	39.5

Sources: 1966: U.S. Equal Employment Opportunity Commission, *Job Patterns for Minorities and Women in Private Industry, 1966*, Report No. 1 (Washington: The Commission, 1968), Part II.
1967: U.S. Equal Employment Opportunity Commission, *Job Patterns for Minorities and Women in Private Industry, 1967*, Report No. 2 (Washington: The Commission, 1970), Vol. I.
1969: U.S. Equal Employment Opportunity Commission.
1970: U.S. Equal Employment Opportunity Commission.

TABLE 38. *Furniture Industry*
Percent Negro Employment by Sex and Occupational Group
Midwest, 1964-1970

Occupational Group	All Employees					Male					Female				
	1964	1966	1967	1969	1970	1964	1966	1967	1969	1970	1964	1966	1967	1969	1970
Officials and managers	0.4	0.4	0.5	0.9	1.4	0.3	0.4	0.5	0.9	1.3	4.3	0.3	0.7	0.6	4.7
Professionals	0.4	0.6	0.3	0.2	0.5	0.4	0.7	0.3	0.2	0.6	—	—	—	—	—
Technicians	0.3	1.1	1.0	1.2	1.0	0.3	1.0	1.0	1.2	1.0	—	2.1	2.0	2.0	0.9
Sales workers	—	—	—	0.2	0.1	—	—	—	0.1	0.1	—	—	—	1.8	—
Office and clerical workers	0.8	1.2	1.8	1.7	1.7	1.5	1.9	2.5	2.3	2.3	0.4	0.8	1.6	1.5	1.5
Total white collar	0.5	0.7	1.1	1.1	1.3	0.5	0.7	0.8	0.9	1.1	0.4	0.8	1.5	1.5	1.5
Craftsmen	4.4	4.9	7.6	6.9	8.6	4.3	4.7	7.5	6.3	7.3	6.0	6.4	8.3	11.3	17.4
Operatives	8.4	9.7	7.8	6.8	7.4	8.2	9.9	8.0	6.7	7.5	9.1	8.7	7.3	7.1	7.2
Laborers	11.7	10.5	11.0	9.7	10.0	10.1	11.5	12.1	10.8	10.1	20.8	7.0	8.7	8.0	9.9
Service workers	18.5	8.0	11.4	10.3	11.0	17.0	7.7	11.6	10.5	10.6	27.0	11.1	10.5	8.9	13.8
Total blue collar	8.5	8.9	8.6	7.7	8.4	8.0	9.1	8.9	7.7	8.1	12.1	7.9	7.9	7.8	9.2
Total	6.2	7.1	7.0	6.1	6.6	6.1	7.5	7.3	6.2	6.5	6.5	5.5	6.1	6.1	6.9

Sources: Appendix Tables A-20 to A-24.

ployment of Negroes, with levels of 23.4 and 2.1 percent, respectively. In contrast, Indiana reported Negro blue collar employment at 2.0 percent and Negro white collar employment at 0.3 percent of total employment. Most of the remaining states were concentrated relatively near the regional percentages. As will be discussed in more detail later, much of the variation in the Midwest is the result of variations in Negro population concentrations. Generally, because of the heavy concentration of blacks in the SMSAs of 250,000 or more population (88.6 percent of the region's 1970 black population) and the rather equally distributed number of furniture jobs, Negroes are somewhat restricted in their employment opportunities.

Although EEOC data show total employment increasing from 1966 to 1969, as the sample took in more establishments, the number of black employees decreased. As in other regions, however, the increase in total employment and the decrease in Negro employment is being causd by an exodus of male labor, principally black, and an increase in female labor, principally white. The exodus of male labor, at least since 1967, is only in blue collar jobs and primarily in the craftsmen and operative categories.

In general, the furniture industry of the Midwest did not provide the Negro with major overall employment gains in the latter half of the 1960s. The number of Negroes in the higher-ranking jobs, however, did increase appreciably. Thus, although by 1970 the EEOC survey was reporting only 4,152 Negroes in the midwestern furniture industry, upgrading of Negroes was occurring.

Illinois

Aided by the Chicago market, the industry in Illinois maintained a relatively stable number of furniture jobs in the 1960s. By 1969 total employment was estimated at 26,700, thereby placing Illinois fifth among states in terms of furniture employment.

Chicago is by far the leading area in the state for furniture manufacturing. As early as 1960 almost four out of every five furniture jobs in Illinois were located in Chicago. This has been particularly advantageous for Negroes, as approximately 85.8 percent of the state's Negro population in 1960 and 86.3 percent of the state's Negro population in 1970 were located in that SMSA. Whereas the 1960 Census reported SMSA and state Negro populations of 14.3 percent and 10.3 percent, respectively, by 1970 these had increased to 17.6 and 12.8 percent. Negro employment is quite high in the industry in Illinois as a result of this overlapping of Negro population concentrations and abundant furniture jobs.

In 1960 the estimate was that 11.2 percent of the state's furniture work force was black. By 1966 firms employing 100 or more workers were reporting a level of 16.3 percent black (Table 39). Between 1966 and 1970 the overall level, although fluctuating somewhat, did not change substantially. Nevertheless, Illinois still ranks second among all top ten furniture states in terms of Negro employment in both the blue collar and white collar categories. Among blue collar jobs, sizable gains have occurred in the craftsmen category, and among white collar jobs, sizable gains have occurred in the officials and managers category.

Indiana

Negroes have not greatly benefited from the Indiana furniture industry. Although the industry employed 25,300 workers in 1969, an increase of approximately 4,300 since 1960, the level of Negro employment continues to be low. Whereas in 1960 Negroes constituted 0.8 percent of the total industry work force, by 1970 the EEOC-based level was only 1.7 percent (Table 40). Until 1969 both the percentage and total figures for employment and Negro employment had shown more impressive gains. With the downturn in the economy in 1970, however, all employment, and particularly Negro employment, was adversely affected. For example, between 1969 and 1970, the number of Negroes employed in firms of 100 or more workers was cut in half—from 566 to 284—as total employment declined from 22,820 to 16,657 (Appendix Tables A-55 to A-56).

The low overall level of Negro employment in the furniture industry in Indiana is reflected in both blue collar and white collar categories. In both categories the Indiana percentages represent the lowest found among the top ten states. In spite of the low levels, a gradual increase in both categories occurred between 1966 and 1969. In 1970, however, this trend stopped. Even in the peak year of 1969 the EEOC survey reported only 21 Negro white collar workers, most of them in clerical positions, and 545 blue collar workers. By 1970 these numbers had dropped to 10 and 274 respectively (Appendix Table A-56).

TABLE 39. *Furniture Industry*
Percent Negro Employment by Sex and Occupational Group
Illinois, 1966-1970

Occupational Group	All Employees				Male				Female			
	1966	1967	1969	1970	1966	1967	1969	1970	1966	1967	1969	1970
Officials and managers	1.0	1.6	2.4	3.8	0.9	1.6	2.5	3.3	2.9	2.7	2.0	12.3
Professionals	0.5	0.9	0.5	0.6	0.6	1.0	0.5	0.7	—	—	—	—
Technicians	0.8	0.9	2.9	1.3	0.8	1.0	2.8	1.5	—	—	3.3	—
Sales workers	—	—	—	—	—	—	—	—	—	—	—	—
Office and clerical workers	2.1	2.5	2.6	2.0	3.7	5.1	6.7	5.4	1.4	1.6	1.5	1.1
Total white collar	1.4	1.8	2.1	2.1	1.3	1.9	2.5	2.5	1.4	1.5	1.5	1.5
Craftsmen	11.1	15.8	19.2	21.0	10.8	16.4	17.1	18.5	12.7	12.8	26.6	28.3
Operatives	24.3	21.2	21.4	21.1	25.0	22.6	21.2	20.8	21.4	17.5	21.8	22.2
Laborers	26.6	27.9	27.1	31.4	28.2	29.0	28.6	30.6	20.9	25.2	24.0	33.8
Service workers	16.4	18.1	24.6	22.4	15.9	18.8	25.2	22.4	21.4	13.8	14.3	21.4
Total blue collar	21.7	21.4	22.5	23.4	22.2	22.3	22.1	22.4	19.7	18.8	23.4	26.7
Total	16.3	16.5	15.6	16.1	17.6	17.8	16.1	16.3	12.1	13.2	14.6	15.5

Sources: Appendix Tables A-45 to A-48.

TABLE 40. *Furniture Industry*

Percent Negro Employment by Sex and Occupational Group
Indiana, 1966-1970

Occupational Group	All Employees				Male				Female			
	1966	1967	1969	1970	1966	1967	1969	1970	1966	1967	1969	1970
Officials and managers	—	0.1	0.4	0.2	—	0.1	0.4	0.2	—	—	—	—
Professionals	—	—	—	—	—	—	—	—	—	—	—	—
Technicians	—	1.0	0.3	0.4	—	1.0	0.4	—	—	—	—	9.1
Sales workers	—	—	—	—	—	—	—	—	—	—	—	—
Office and clerical workers	0.3	0.2	0.8	0.5	0.3	—	—	0.3	0.2	0.2	1.1	0.6
Total white collar	0.1	0.2	0.5	0.3	0.1	0.1	0.2	0.2	0.2	0.2	1.0	0.6
Craftsmen	0.8	1.0	1.7	1.3	0.8	1.0	1.7	1.3	0.9	1.3	2.1	1.3
Operatives	2.2	2.0	2.8	1.7	1.7	1.7	2.5	1.6	3.8	2.9	3.4	1.8
Laborers	1.1	2.4	3.3	2.8	1.4	3.4	3.7	1.5	0.4	0.6	2.8	4.9
Service workers	3.2	6.0	8.0	4.5	2.2	5.5	8.2	3.3	10.3	9.3	7.4	16.1
Total blue collar	1.6	2.0	2.9	2.0	1.4	2.0	2.8	1.6	2.4	2.0	3.1	3.0
Total	1.4	1.7	2.5	1.7	1.2	1.8	2.4	1.3	1.9	1.7	2.7	2.6

Sources: Appendix Tables A-53 to A-56.

Although the state has a relatively small Negro population (6.9 percent of the total population in 1970), the lack of employment opportunities for Negroes is made worse by the internal mismatching of areas of furniture employment and Negro population concentration. For example, in 1960 only 8.0 percent of total furniture employment was found in SMSAs of 250,000 or more population. In contrast, 69.5 percent of the Negro population was found in those areas. By 1970 this population concentration had increased to 80.4 percent, thereby further reducing employment opportunities for blacks. Thus, it is not surprising that there is a low level of Negro employment in the Indiana industry.

In spite of the fact that the total number of men and the number of Negro men continued to increase until 1969, the Indiana work force has become increasingly composed of women. In 1966 approximately 22 percent of the work force were women; by 1970 the level was 31 percent. For the most part the shift is occurring in the blue collar categories, particularly among operatives and laborers, where it is relatively easier for men to switch to somewhat similar jobs in better-paying industries.

Michigan

Although less than fifty years ago Michigan was among the top two or three furniture-producing states in the country, it had dropped to seventh place in terms of total furniture employment by 1960 and to ninth place by 1969. During the 1960s total furniture employment remained relatively stable, and by 1969 was reported to be 21,500.

The 1960s, although seeing some progress for Negroes in the Michigan furniture industry, was not a period of great advancement. Whereas in 1960 Negro employment represented 3.8 percent of total furniture employment, by 1970 the level, based on EEOC data, was 5.7 percent (Table 41). Among the top ten states in furniture employment this level ranked ninth, a ranking that was true for both blue collar and white collar categories. Since 1966 the number of Negro men in blue collar categories has declined by 240, primarily among laborers and operatives, in spite of a slight increase in total male blue collar employment. However, both the total number of women, and the number of black women, in blue collar jobs have increased.

TABLE 41. *Furniture Industry*
Percent Negro Employment by Sex and Occupational Group
Michigan, 1966-1970

Occupational Group	All Employees				Male				Female			
	1966	1967	1969	1970	1966	1967	1969	1970	1966	1967	1969	1970
Officials and managers	0.9	0.2	0.4	0.5	0.9	0.2	0.5	0.5	—	—	—	—
Professionals	0.4	0.4	—	0.9	0.4	0.4	—	0.9	—	—	—	—
Technicians	0.4	0.5	1.8	1.4	0.4	0.5	1.9	1.5	—	—	—	—
Sales workers	—	—	0.2	0.4	—	—	0.3	0.5	—	—	—	—
Office and clerical workers	0.7	0.9	1.1	1.8	1.5	1.6	0.8	1.4	0.3	0.6	1.2	1.9
Total white collar	0.6	0.5	0.8	1.1	0.7	0.5	0.6	0.8	0.3	0.6	1.0	1.7
Craftsmen	2.6	3.4	4.4	3.9	2.0	3.3	4.2	3.7	7.4	4.6	6.8	7.2
Operatives	10.7	6.2	6.6	7.6	10.8	5.6	6.2	7.0	10.0	8.9	8.9	10.2
Laborers	10.1	9.4	10.4	8.8	10.2	8.4	8.5	6.5	9.6	11.5	13.5	12.4
Service workers	1.7	5.4	5.6	7.0	1.2	5.0	5.4	8.0	12.5	7.8	6.5	2.3
Total blue collar	8.9	6.3	7.3	7.3	8.8	5.6	6.2	6.2	9.5	9.5	11.0	11.2
Total	7.1	5.0	5.7	5.7	7.3	4.6	5.0	5.0	6.4	6.6	7.9	8.0

Sources: Appendix Tables A-61 to A-64.

Although there has been relatively little progress in blue collar employment, white collar employment has fared somewhat better. Both the total number of men and the number of Negro men in white collar employment have increased among firms of 100 or more employees. In addition, the figures for all women and for Negro women in white collar employment have also increased. However, no Negro women are as yet employed in any nonclerical white collar jobs. In spite of the lack of major improvements in white collar employment for Negroes, Michigan has three Negro professionals and two Negro sales workers in the industry's work force. In these two white collar categories the state is unsurpassed by any of the other ten major states.

On the surface it would seem that because approximately half of Michigan's furniture employment is concentrated in the state's major SMSAs and because approximately 86 percent of the state's 1970 Negro population is concentrated there also, a relatively larger number of Negroes would be employed in the industry. On closer examination, however, it is found that approximately one-third of the state's furniture employment is in Grand Rapids—an SMSA with a Negro population of only 4 percent. Thus, even though the concentration of furniture employment and Negro population may be in the SMSAs of the state, there is no overlapping that would work to the Negro's advantage.

Ohio

Ohio's status as a major furniture state has declined somewhat in recent years. Whereas in 1960 it ranked eighth in terms of employment, in the past decade it has not kept pace with other states and currently ranks tenth. Such developments have not contributed to any spectacular employment gains for Negroes. In 1960 Negroes made up 4.7 percent of total furniture employment in the state and by 1970 the level, based on EEOC data, was only 6.6 percent—a level that had not substantially changed since at least 1966 (Table 42).

In spite of the lack of spectacular employment gains, there has been some upgrading of blacks in the Ohio industry. Because of a gradual increase in the number of Negro clerical employees and managers, blacks in white collar employment have increased both their numbers and relative percentages. Although white collar gains have occurred, Negroes have lost

TABLE 42.　*Furniture Industry*

Percent Negro Employment by Sex and Occupational Group

Ohio, 1966-1970

Occupational Group	All Employees				Male				Female			
	1966	1967	1969	1970	1966	1967	1969	1970	1966	1967	1969	1970
Officials and managers	0.2	0.2	0.5	1.1	0.2	0.3	0.5	1.2	—	—	—	—
Professionals	1.0	—	0.7	0.5	1.1	—	0.7	0.6	—	—	—	—
Technicians	2.1	2.6	0.7	1.6	1.9	2.3	0.7	1.7	6.3	9.1	—	—
Sales workers	—	—	—	—	—	—	—	—	—	—	—	—
Office and clerical workers	1.3	4.6	2.5	2.7	0.9	3.3	2.2	1.2	1.5	5.2	2.6	3.1
Total white collar	0.8	2.3	1.3	1.6	0.6	1.1	0.7	1.0	1.2	4.9	2.4	2.9
Craftsmen	6.7	11.3	7.5	8.8	6.8	11.3	7.6	8.8	5.3	11.4	6.6	8.1
Operatives	6.9	8.7	6.8	6.7	7.1	9.8	6.7	6.6	5.8	3.9	7.3	7.0
Laborers	14.1	8.8	10.4	11.1	15.2	10.5	11.1	14.5	8.0	1.9	7.9	5.9
Service workers	16.5	22.2	19.6	26.8	17.4	22.0	18.2	25.0	6.7	23.5	30.0	36.4
Total blue collar	9.1	9.7	8.2	8.3	9.5	10.6	8.3	8.7	6.4	4.7	7.8	7.1
Total	6.7	7.8	6.4	6.6	7.4	8.5	6.5	6.9	3.8	4.8	5.7	5.6

Sources:　Appendix Tables A-65 to A-68.

some ground in the blue collar areas since 1966, but these losses have been primarily in the lower-ranking jobs.

The decline in the number of Negroes in the blue collar areas is largely the result of female labor replacing male labor. As blue collar male workers, both black and white, have left the Ohio industry, they have been replaced by women, and the majority of these women have been white. The Negro women who are employed continue to be hired almost exclusively for blue collar jobs or for clerical positions.

The Ohio furniture industry is rather heavily concentrated in several large urban areas of the state. Since the Negro population is heavily concentrated in the large SMSAs (91.2 percent in 1970), and particularly in the largest ones, almost all Negroes found in the state's industry are employed in these areas. Consequently, black furniture employment levels in cities like Cincinnati and Cleveland tend to be high, while nonurban areas and some middle-size cities report relatively low levels.

WEST

The West, like the South and Midwest, encompasses more than one region. In Department of Labor statistics the area is frequently divided into the Pacific and the Mountain states. Since more than 90 percent of regional furniture employment is found in the Pacific states the discussion here will deal primarily with this area.

Although the western furniture industry, in comparison to other regions, was relatively late in starting, it accounted for 11.1 percent of industry employment as of 1960. Although the region has continued to attract new plants, the growth rate has not matched that of the South and so its percentage of national furniture employment has declined slightly, to 10.8 percent as of 1969.

Whereas the percentage of Negro employment in western furniture-manufacturing firms of 100 or more workers exceeded all nonsouthern regions through 1967, in more recent years the percentage has declined (Table 43) as other regions either increased or remained relatively stable. Thus, by 1969 the West had been surpassed by the Middle Atlantic region and was being closely challenged by the Midwest. The decline in percentage as well as a slight drop in the total number of black employees have occurred despite the fact that total employment,

TABLE 43. *Furniture Industry*
Percent Negro Employment by Sex and Occupational Group
West (Pacific), 1964-1969

Occupational Group	All Employees				Male				Female			
	1964	1966	1967	1969	1964	1966	1967	1969	1964	1966	1967	1969
Officials and managers	—	1.6	1.7	1.5	—	1.6	1.7	1.6	—	—	—	—
Professionals	—	—	4.2	1.0	—	—	4.5	1.1	—	—	—	—
Technicians	10.0	4.8	6.1	3.7	10.3	5.2	5.1	4.2	—	—	25.0	—
Sales workers	—	—	—	0.2	—	—	—	0.2	—	—	—	—
Office and clerical workers	1.3	2.3	2.4	1.3	1.0	4.5	5.2	1.8	1.4	1.4	1.1	1.2
Total white collar	1.1	1.7	2.0	1.3	1.0	2.0	2.4	1.4	1.3	1.2	1.1	1.0
Craftsmen	3.8	6.6	6.2	6.0	3.8	6.8	6.4	5.6	3.7	5.9	5.2	8.5
Operatives	11.4	11.1	14.7	10.8	11.0	12.1	16.5	11.8	13.2	7.1	7.3	5.9
Laborers	5.4	21.9	9.8	10.3	5.9	25.4	11.3	11.8	—	3.9	3.3	6.1
Service workers	41.0	20.3	14.5	12.7	51.6	21.7	14.2	12.4	—	—	25.0	14.3
Total blue collar	10.1	12.4	11.5	9.5	9.9	13.9	12.8	10.2	11.0	6.1	5.8	6.4
Total	8.1	10.0	9.5	7.8	8.3	11.6	11.0	8.7	7.1	4.4	4.3	4.6

Sources: Appendix Tables A-25 to A-28.

as reported by the EEOC, has increased appreciably since 1966. Such declines, however, have only affected Negro men, and are principally felt in the clerical and operative positions. Although the number of Negro women has continued to increase, they are almost exclusively found in blue collar jobs with a few being employed in clerical positions.

The furniture industry in the West, and particularly in the Pacific region, is heavily concentrated in the large SMSAs where Negro population is also heavily concentrated, thereby eliminating one possible obstacle to increasing the level of Negro employment. Although there were no major gains for Negroes in this region in the latter 1960s, the percentage of Negro employment in the industry is still above the 1970 regional black population level of 4.9 percent.

California

Seventy-seven percent of the region's employment in furniture manufacturing is located in California. Because of the large market for furniture on the West Coast, employment in California has continued to grow in recent years. As of 1969, 37,900 furniture workers were employed in the state, making it the second ranking state in total employment.

In California, furniture manufacturing is almost entirely an urban industry. For example, as early as 1960, 96.3 percent of the state's employment was in the urban areas, with Los Angeles being the dominant SMSA, accounting for more than 70 percent of state employment, and San Francisco ranking a distant second. This industry concentration has worked to the advantage of Negroes, since almost 80 percent of the state's Negro population has been located in these two SMSAs for more than a decade. Together these two SMSAs account for almost 95 percent of the state's Negro employment in furniture manufacturing.

The early 1960s showed progress in Negro employment in the state's industry. For example, in 1960 the level of black employment was estimated to be 4.3 percent. By 1966 EEOC data was indicating a level of 10.0 percent. From a high of 11.0 percent in 1967 the level has dropped to 8.9 percent in 1970 (Table 44). Nevertheless, this percentage continues to be above the 1970 black population level of 7.0 percent.

TABLE 44. *Furniture Industry*
Percent Negro Employment by Sex and Occupational Group
California, 1966-1970

Occupational Group	All Employees				Male				Female			
	1966	1967	1969	1970	1966	1967	1969	1970	1966	1967	1969	1970
Officials and managers	1.6	1.9	1.9	2.1	1.6	2.0	1.9	2.2	—	—	—	—
Professionals	—	4.3	1.1	1.6	—	4.7	1.2	0.9	—	—	—	7.7
Technicians	4.8	6.3	4.5	5.6	5.2	5.3	5.1	5.1	—	25.0	—	11.1
Sales workers	—	—	0.2	0.2	—	—	0.3	0.2	—	—	—	—
Office and clerical workers	2.3	2.6	1.5	2.0	4.5	5.6	2.0	2.3	1.4	1.2	1.3	1.9
Total white collar	1.7	2.2	1.5	1.9	2.0	2.7	1.7	1.9	1.2	1.2	1.2	1.9
Craftsmen	6.6	7.2	7.0	7.4	6.8	7.5	6.6	6.6	5.9	5.8	10.5	13.3
Operatives	11.1	16.5	12.7	12.1	12.1	18.5	13.8	12.9	7.1	8.1	7.1	9.1
Laborers	21.9	12.8	16.5	12.1	25.4	14.5	17.0	13.7	3.9	4.7	14.2	5.0
Service workers	20.3	14.7	12.9	10.9	21.7	14.4	13.1	9.5	—	33.3	11.5	33.3
Total blue collar	12.4	13.5	12.1	10.8	13.9	15.0	12.6	11.3	6.1	6.9	9.5	8.9
Total	10.0	11.0	9.7	8.9	11.6	12.7	10.6	9.5	4.4	4.9	6.3	6.5

Sources: Appendix Tables A-33 to A-36.

COMPANY EXPERIENCES

The impact of Negro population concentration on **Negro** employment is particularly evident at the company level. Outside the South, except for large metropolitan areas, it is relatively unusual to find black furniture workers. For example, two nonmetropolitan northeastern companies visited for this study had no Negroes employed in any of their operations. The maximum that had ever been employed in either plant at one time was two. Since the black community represents only 1 percent of total population, and the companies have not expanded in recent years,[155] the lack of black employment is not surprising. A similar situation exists in many midwestern furniture operations. One Michigan firm reported that although they had been the first manufacturer in their area to employ Negroes, they had never employed more than two and they had never been employed at levels higher than operatives. Again, this company had not expanded greatly in recent years and was located in an area with a black population of approximately 0.1 percent.[156]

If a firm has locations throughout the country, it is quite likely that its various plants will reflect the community population distribution. One large firm headquartered in the Midwest reported plants in large urban centers of the Midwest and West which employed relatively high percentages of blacks. In contrast, their plants in relatively nonurban areas had few blacks. In their southern plants, employment again varied according to the population. In spite of this company's relatively large number of employees and wide dispersion of plant locations, they too had experienced difficulty in finding Negro white collar employees. Only recently had they employed their first Negro professional, and they still had no Negro sales workers.[157]

Among many of the major southern manufacturers it is not unusual to find firms that have long employed blacks, but only in the past decade have begun upgrading them. One such company, although employing in 1966 a work force of approximately 750 blacks—a black employment level of 20 percent—reported having only 10 blacks above the level of operatives, 1 being a clerical employee and 9 being craftsmen. With gradual in-

---

155. Interview, January 1972.

156. Interview, January 1972.

157. Interview, April 1972.

creases each year, the company as of 1971 was employing more than 80 black craftsmen, approximately 15 black clerical employees and either 1 or 2 black employees in all other white collar jobs except sales workers. The improvement in this company resulted from conscious efforts on the part of management. By developing training programs and working with community programs they have not only upgraded blacks but have also continued to employ increasing numbers of blacks in their total work force. Thus, although the company is primarily located in a community with a black population of 20 percent, the Negro employment level currently approaches 30 percent.[158]

Another southern firm, by using such programs as education subsidies and by supporting community training programs, has increased the number of Negroes in craftsmen and higher-ranking categories from 100 in 1966 (all male craftsmen) to 226 in 1971. By 1971, in addition to 167 male and 54 female black craftsmen, there were 5 blacks in white collar jobs: 3 clericals, 1 manager and 1 professional. By contrast, in 1966 there had been no Negro white collar employees.[159]

Although most of the large furniture manufacturers native to the South have long employed Negroes in some capacity, some firms that have migrated into the South have not employed Negroes until recent years. One such firm reported that although it employed several hundred workers it was not until the mid-1960s that they began to employ Negroes. Such a decision, rather than resulting from civil rights pressure, came about because of a tight labor market created by new industries moving into the area. At present that same company has a work force that is approximately 20 percent black—a level that is slightly above the black population percentage in the community.[160]

SUMMARY

Although passage of the 1964 Civil Rights Act created an increased awareness of discriminatory practices in the furniture industry, it was principally the three factors of industry growth, skill levels, and location which combined during the decade to

---

158. Interview, January 1972.

159. Interview, December 1971.

160. Interview, June 1972.

produce a period of growing employment for Negroes. As the economy expanded and personal incomes increased, consumer demands for furniture reached new highs. This product demand brought on greater industry demand for labor, which, when combined with the heavy concentration of the industry in the South, opened up an increasing number of jobs for all members of the southern labor force, both black and white. As other industries expanded in the South, a large portion of the white male labor force rejected furniture manufacturing for higher-paying industries. Consequently, the furniture industry turned increasingly to what were once considered marginal workers. As a result, increasing numbers of Negroes and women, many without previous industrial work experience, were employed.

During the 1960s two trends emerged which, if continued, will slow down the rate of Negro furniture employment. The first is a migration phenomenon. Between 1960 and 1970 there was a distinct movement of Negroes out of the South. Whereas in 1960, 59.1 percent of the total Negro population of the United States was in the South, by 1970 the figure was only 53.0 percent. This meant that Negroes dropped from 20.1 percent to 19.1 percent of the South's population as all other regions were increasing their levels by at least one percentage point. In addition to the movement of blacks from the South, an important movement within the South was occurring—the increased urbanization of Negroes. Whereas in 1960 only 30.4 percent of southern blacks lived in SMSAs of 250,000 or more population, by 1970 the level had increased to 40.6 percent. All other regions either remained relatively stable or increased their concentration by only four percentage points or less.

The second trend was the continuing concentration of the furniture industry in the South, particularly in the more rural portions of the region. Whereas in 1960 the South claimed 138,400 furniture workers, or approximately 37 percent of national employment, by 1969 the figures had increased to 192,500, or 42.3 percent. The net result of these two trends is that Negroes are moving away from the areas of high furniture employment.

Because much of the Negro migration is to urban centers outside the South, particularly to such cities as New York, Philadelphia, Chicago, and Los Angeles, all of which are furniture-manufacturing centers, it seems likely that furniture employment in these cities will continue to become increasingly black. Since, however, some of these cities are declining in importance in terms of furniture manufacturing, the long-term prospects for blacks are probably not as good as they would have been had they remained in the South.

The above trends not only work against increasing the levels of Negroes in furniture manufacturing; they are also creating serious problems for the industry. Because it is labor intensive, the industry has traditionally relied on a large source of relatively inexpensive labor to man its plants. Now, one such source is declining. This situation has prompted some leading companies to consider ways to reduce the exodus of Negroes. No tangible proposals, however, have yet been implemented.

The past decade was a period during which employment opportunities for Negroes increased in a way unparalleled in the furniture industry's history. If present trends continue, it seems unlikely that the 1970s will match the growth of the 1960s. Nevertheless, as long as blacks remain available for furniture employment, there is little doubt but that employment opportunities will exist for them. As one industry executive stated, "We simply can't afford to discriminate." [161]

---

161. Interview, March 1972.

CHAPTER VI

Some Problems of Equal Opportunity

Although the passage of civil rights legislation and the issuance of equal opportunity-oriented executive orders made necessary a change in the practices and policies of some furniture manufacturers, relatively few problems have resulted. Some adjustment problems did occur in individual situations, but for the most part there were apparently few problems that approached universality.

EMPLOYMENT PROBLEMS

There seems to have been a fairly universal acceptance of Negroes into the work force of most furniture plants. Since some plants have employed Negroes since their beginning and have gradually increased their percentage of Negro employment over the years, the passage of civil rights legislation brought few major employment changes. The gradual addition of more blacks, when combined with an expanding demand for labor, resulted in relatively little jealousy on the part of whites.

There have been some instances in various furniture companies of Negroes filing EEOC complaints charging discrimination in promotions and discharges. Such situations, however, are relatively rare. Whereas Negroes may have once been the first to be laid off and the last to be promoted, such practices are now generally nonexistant, as the concepts of seniority and merit have become more widespread in the industry.

Although not as common as cases of blacks complaining of discrimination, there have been instances of whites filing charges of reverse discrimination. In addition, there have been cases of blacks complaining to company officials over the promotion of other blacks into supervisory positions. In general, however, such situations are rare.

An additional problem associated with the increased employment of blacks is the seeming existence of an inverse relationship between the level of Negro employment in the plant and the number of applications from whites after a certain ratio of blacks to whites is reached. Because few plants have extremely high ratios of black-to-white employment, this has not become a widespread problem. There are, however, a few isolated cases of plants that previously had quite high ratios of Negro employment becoming completely black in makeup.

As in some other industries, the relative scarcity of skilled Negroes willing to work in the furniture industry is a problem. Although the furniture industry employs relatively few skilled workers, there is a need for some, particularly in the white collar jobs. Because of such factors as the general scarcity of highly skilled Negroes, the availability of higher salaries in other industries and the reluctance of some qualified Negroes to seek employment in many rural furniture centers, furniture companies continue to report low levels of Negro employment in such categories. According to one industrial relations executive, "White collar jobs in furniture will be held by Negroes when Negroes are both qualified and available."[162] Thus far, these two conditions have not been sufficiently met.

INTEGRATION OF FACILITIES

When handled improperly, the integration of company facilities can create major problems. Generally, the furniture companies that have taken a firm position and combined that with an accurate explanation of the reasons for integration have faced few problems. The furniture representatives interviewed in this study, almost without exception, indicated that they had experienced little or no problem over the integration of facilities by following such a policy, whether those facilities included cafeterias, drinking fountains, locker rooms, restrooms, or recreational facilities.

Some companies, both in the South and elsewhere, have never maintained segregated facilities, and so the passage of civil rights legislation created no new accommodation problems for them. Because of their size, most companies do not have cafeterias or locker rooms. In addition, some of the larger com-

---

162. Interview, January 1972.

panies, who in recent years have built cafeterias, have always operated them on an integrated basis and have encountered no difficulty.

The Civil Rights Act did force many furniture companies to eliminate segregated restrooms and water fountains—the most common form of segregated facilities. For the most part, such action did not result in any appreciable trouble. In a few situations a small percentage of the white work force did voice opposition by means of petitions and signs. In such cases management generally responded by meeting with the protest group to explain the company's position and the supportive reasons. After such meetings the protesters either gave up their opposition or resigned.

Although it was once fairly common for major companies to provide housing for employees, almost all companies have given up this practice. This action not only reduced administrative problems and costs but also eliminated a potentially sensitive employee relations problem.

EFFICIENCY AND TURNOVER

It has frequently been argued that if employers hire too many Negroes the efficiency of their operations will decline because of the assumed lack of reliability of Negroes. As noted in Chapter III, this early obstacle to Negro employment in the furniture industry was primarily overcome during World War II.

On an individual basis there are undoubtedly cases in which Negro labor has proven undependable, but this is true of white labor as well. Particularly in cases in which an employee is experiencing his first industrial assignment, a situation not uncommon for many Negroes in southern furniture plants, there may be an initial adjustment period in which pay checks received on Friday lead to long weekends. A few companies visited for this study reported such a problem among some of their black employees. To deal with this problem, certain companies have developed training and orientation programs that emphasize personal motivation as well as job-related skills.

Most companies visited indicated no difference between the dependability of black and white labor, particularly in regard to employee turnover. The only difference in dependability discernible to many was found between young and older employees of all races. The high turnover rate experienced by the furniture industry is not an across-the-board problem, but seems to occur most often in only 10 to 20 percent of the jobs, most of the turnover coming from young workers who are undecided as to career goals. Another source of turnover problems in the more rural areas of the South is the seasonal worker. It is not unusual for some furniture workers to combine their furniture jobs with farming; consequently, in the spring and fall turnover rates increase for some companies as regional crops are planted and harvested.

GOVERNMENT PRESSURE

Although government influence in the area of civil rights has aided the goal of equal employment, it has created some difficulties for a number of companies. The major complaint is the government's seeming insistence on results as measured by employment percentages instead of a more realistic view of each particular situation. A number of company representatives expressed the feeling that the government, in its great concern for demonstrable results, has often been unaware of extenuating circumstances, such as the availability of Negro labor, particularly for white collar jobs. For example, one nonsouthern plant without Negro employees reported receiving considerable pressure from the government to employ Negroes, although there were virtually no Negroes in the entire community.

An additional problem reported by some companies was the easy availability of EEOC machinery which, they felt, tends to create a demand for its services. Some companies which, until the last year or so, had never been the subject of employee discrimination complaints, have in recent years been the subject of an increasing number of them. Whether this is the result of problems that have always existed but went unreported, or whether government influence is encouraging meritless complaints, is unresolved. A number of industry representatives believe, however, that the latter is most often the case.

Although most industry representatives feel that the government's civil rights influence has not reduced efficiency, there is in some states the belief that government aid programs have hindered employee recruitment efforts. Because of the relatively high rates of unemployment compensation and welfare payment in some states and the relatively low wage rates paid by the furniture industry, it is felt by some that potential workers are encouraged to reject opportunities to do furniture work.

Such government requirements as affirmative action plans, compliance reviews, and EEOC reports do not seem to have created too many problems for the typical furniture company. When industry executives feel, however, that the various equal employment programs are being administered inequitably, then they see the influence of the government as being a source of problems.

SUMMARY

In general, the furniture industry in recent years has experienced relatively few problems in regard to equal employment opportunities. The problems that have arisen, for the most part, have been rather isolated. Neither resentment by white workers to the employment and advancement of qualified Negroes nor the desegregation of facilities have been industry problems. The basic advantages of the furniture industry over some other industries in this regard have been its rapid expansion and its resulting need for labor.

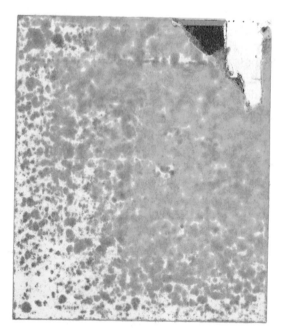

CHAPTER VII

Determinants of Industrial Policy

The current status of Negro employment in the furniture industry is attributable to several factors working in combination. Although these factors have been alluded to throughout this study, they are discussed in detail in this chapter.

THE DEMAND FOR LABOR

Negroes have made their greatest employment gains in periods of labor shortage. Historically, a constant supply of European immigrants and later an abundance of white male labor in furniture-manufacturing centers made the employment of any appreciable number of Negroes unnecessary. As long as the supply of white workers exceeded the industry's demand for labor, Negroes remained largely excluded from employment opportunities.

During the twentieth century other industries, often paying higher wages, moved into areas previously dominated by the furniture industry. It became necessary for furniture manufacturers either to pay competitive wages or to employ more marginal workers at less than competitive rates. Because the industry is both labor intensive and highly competitive, the latter alternative was generally pursued. Thus, in areas where Negroes were concentrated and unable to compete successfully with whites for jobs in the better-paying industries, they were increasingly employed by the furniture industry.

The World War II and postwar periods highlighted the impact of economic conditions on furniture industry employment. With the relative scarcity of labor created by wartime manpower needs and later by an expanding economy, an increasing number of Negroes and women found employment in furniture manufacturing. Whereas white male labor was often readily hired by higher-paying industries, Negroes and women had to be content with lower-paying industries, such as furniture.

Because of the continued demand for furniture and the increasing scarcity of alternative sources of cheap labor, the furniture industry is approaching a crucial stage in its history. To solve its manpower needs, the most likely alternatives are either to pay more competitive wages so as to retain labor, or to increase automation. Although some companies are exploring the possibility of using job enrichment as a means of dealing with their problems, a realistic forecast for the near future would be a combination of increased wages and automation, with a greater inclination toward higher wages. Although increased automation is being considered by a number of prominent firms, any major development is still quite far from implementation. Thus, for the near future, employment opportunities for Negroes will continue to exist, provided that there is a continued availability of black labor and a strong demand for furniture.

JOB STRUCTURE

The job structure in most furniture-manufacturing plants has worked to the advantage of Negroes. Although in the early days of the industry labor was highly skilled and almost artistic in nature, since the advent of power machinery the necessary skill level has dropped drastically. At present the work level is semi-skilled, at best, and many jobs are performed by unskilled labor. Because of the current job structure, no appreciable skill barrier exists for Negroes or any other prospective applicants. When the lack of skill barriers is combined with a growing industry, it is inevitable that labor excluded from employment in other industries will find employment in furniture. Thus, in many areas Negroes have been able to increase substantially their levels of employment in the furniture industry.

As discussed earlier, increased automation is much more widely discussed than practiced. It seems inevitable, however, that increased automation will occur in the future. Many industry representatives feel that such a development, although raising industry skill levels, will not affect blacks any more severely than whites. They point out that such automation will result in only slightly increased skill levels and that any gap that may currently exist between the education and skills of blacks and whites will be appreciably narrowed, if not eliminated, by educational changes.

PLANT LOCATION

The location of furniture-manufacturing plants has been a key factor in the increasing level of Negro employment. As discussed in Chapter V, the variation in Negro employment levels between regions, states, and cities is closely related to population variations. Not until the furniture industry began moving to the South were any appreciable number of blacks employed. As the industry grew in the South, Negro employment continued to increase until by 1970 the national level of Negro employment in the industry was estimated at approximately 13 percent.

In general, locational considerations have been one of the greatest single factors, if not the greatest factor, contributing to the increased levels of Negro employment. The combination of this factor with a growing demand for labor and the relative lack of skills necessary for furniture employment seems to explain the change in the racial makeup of total furniture employment during the 1960s.

GOVERNMENT PRESSURE

As indicated earlier most furniture companies have been virtually immune from government pressure. Because of their size and the absence of government contracts, most furniture manufacturers have remained outside EEOC and OFCC jurisdiction. Even the larger firms that are involved in contract work have been, for the most part, unaffected.

In a few situations direct pressure has been applied by such means as Justice Department suits, compliance reviews, and affirmative action plans. Such actions, although affecting the isolated situations, have had relatively little impact on the total level of Negro employment in the furniture industry. Direct pressures, however, have had a broad effect on improving employment opportunities for blacks. The principal contribution of government pressures has been the fostering of an increased awareness of minority employment problems, particularly promotional discrimination, and a resolve to correct such problems.

After the passage of the 1964 Civil Rights Act, it was not unusual for furniture companies to inspect carefully their operation so as to eliminate obvious discriminatory practices. The result was the desegregation of such facilities as restrooms, cafeterias, and water fountains. In addition, attention was given, often for the first time, to upgrading minorities as well as to developing a companywide attitude of respect for all employees. A major element in the latter development was the incorporation of sessions on civil rights into supervisory training programs. In general, the role of the government in the furniture industry has been a positive one in that it has forced many companies into efforts in self-examination designed to correct their own problems before being forced to do so by the government.

UNIONISM AND SENIORITY

Because of the highly fragmented nature of the furniture industry and the relatively large number of unions in it, no single union has established a dominant industry position. In fact, the majority of the work force continues to be nonunion. Consequently, no union has been able to exert a substantial influence on racial policies of the industry. Except for an occasional equal employment opportunity provision in a union constitution or contract signed before the Civil Rights Act, unions in the furniture industry have had little or no effect on the employment of Negroes.

As might be expected in a relatively nonunionized industry, the seniority system is often not rigidly defined. Although it is a factor that is considered in most promotion and layoff situations, seniority generally is not the basis upon which such decisions are made; instead, ability tends to be the major criterion. Many industry representatives view the lack of a controlling seniority system as a factor facilitating the upgrading of minorities. Although many Negroes have only recently been employed in some furniture plants, this does not necessarily put them at a disadvantage in terms of promotion opportunities.

MANAGEMENT POLICY

Although a few furniture companies developed written equal employment opportunity policies prior to the Civil Rights Act of 1964, the vast majority currently having such a policy developed them after the Act was passed. At present most companies display their policy through such means as application forms, employment advertisements and bulletin board notices.

Only recently have many furniture manufacturers recognized the need to assume social responsibilities. Because of the relatively small size of most furniture plants and the lack of consumer orientation to specific manufacturers, furniture has been a low visibility industry. Consequently, it has received little pressure to accept social responsibilities. At least two factors have contributed to a current increase in the awareness of social responsibilities. First, some manufacturers are increasing their public visibility by such means as direct advertising, participation in industrywide promotional programs such as "Debut 1972," and opening their own retail outlets. Second, public visibility is being enhanced by organizational changes such as mergers and the entry of conglomerates into the industry.

Conglomerates seem particularly aware of the need for a good reputation in the area of equal employment. Not only are they concerned with the public relations aspect of the issue, but they are also more likely to contract with the government. Because of the multiplicity of products involved there are likely to be some areas within the conglomerate in which sizable government contracts exist. Even though the furniture division may do no contract work, it becomes subject to compliance requirements by virtue of its being a part of the conglomerate. Because of this development, some furniture companies which have become divisions of large parent organizations find themselves required to submit annual affirmative action plans with numerical goals. For example, one furniture company found itself not only subject to annual affirmative action plans but also to annual presentations before corporate executives. Good performance in its equal employment program was considered to be as important as good performance in the areas of finance and safety.[163]

Since conglomerates often have industrial relations personnel working solely in the area of equal employment opportunity, they are able to provide some leadership and direction to furniture companies that previously had little expertise in the area. Because many furniture companies employed large numbers of blacks before being purchased, the leadership and direction of conglomerates has been principally evident in the area of upgrading. If the conglomerate movement continues into the future, it can be expected that upgrading will become an increasingly important management policy for the furniture industry.

---

163. Interview, March 1972.

CONCLUDING REMARKS

Since the turn of the century Negroes have constituted a discernible portion of the furniture industry's work force. Until the 1960s almost all Negro employment was located in the lower blue collar jobs. During the 1960s, however, the level of black employment increased at a rate in excess of that for previous decades and blacks also began to be upgraded to a greater extent than ever before. Although such advances were stimulated in part by the federal government's civil rights activities, they were more the result of labor market conditions. In spite of these recent advances Negroes continue to be heavily concentrated in blue collar jobs.

The prospects for the furniture industry in the near future appear to be good. Whereas the 1971 manufacturers' shipments of household furniture were estimated at $6.1 billion, the projection for 1975 is for shipments in excess of $8 billion, an increase of more than 7 percent each year during the period from 1971 to 1975. By 1980 household furniture shipments should be approximately $10.6 billion, an average annual increase of more than 6 percent.[164]

Since household furniture is the dominant sector in the furniture industry, the prospects for continued growth in furniture employment appear good. Consequently, employment opportunities for Negroes will also continue to be good. Because of labor market factors, the level of Negro employment in the South and in nonsouthern urban areas will probably continue to increase; the extent of such increases will depend primarily upon the availability of other job opportunities and the degree of automation. It also seems likely that in areas of heavy Negro population concentrations, white men will continue to be drawn away from furniture manufacturing, thereby leaving an increasing number of jobs for Negroes.

---

164. U.S. Department of Commerce, *U.S. Industrial Outlook, 1972*, (Washington: U.S. Government Printing Office, 1972), pp. 107-110.

Appendix

GENERAL STATISTICAL INFORMATION

TABLE A-1. *Furniture Industry*

Employment by Race, Sex, and Occupational Group

105 Establishments, United States, 1964

Occupational Group	All Employees			Male			Female		
	Total	Negro	Percent Negro	Total	Negro	Percent Negro	Total	Negro	Percent Negro
Officials and managers	2,206	8	0.4	2,159	7	0.3	47	1	2.1
Professionals	701	2	0.3	670	2	0.3	31	—	—
Technicians	851	4	0.5	814	4	0.5	37	—	—
Sales workers	1,419	—	—	1,376	—	—	43	—	—
Office and clerical workers	4,266	58	1.4	1,334	27	2.0	2,932	31	1.1
Total white collar	9,443	72	0.8	6,353	40	0.6	3,090	32	1.0
Craftsmen	5,845	233	4.0	5,498	212	3.9	347	21	6.1
Operatives	15,943	1,484	9.3	13,619	1,261	9.3	2,324	223	9.6
Laborers	9,616	706	7.3	8,205	612	7.5	1,411	94	6.7
Service workers	694	156	22.5	622	135	21.7	72	21	29.2
Total blue collar	32,098	2,579	8.0	27,944	2,220	7.9	4,154	359	8.6
Total	41,541	2,651	6.4	34,297	2,260	6.6	7,244	391	5.4

Source: Data in author's possession.

TABLE A-2. *Furniture Industry*
Employment by Race, Sex, and Occupational Group
978 Establishments, United States, 1966

Occupational Group	All Employees			Male			Female		
	Total	Negro	Percent Negro	Total	Negro	Percent Negro	Total	Negro	Percent Negro
Officials and manager	15,547	83	0.5	14,850	80	0.5	697	3	0.4
Professionals	3,135	20	0.6	2,970	20	0.7	165	—	—
Technicians	2,949	27	0.9	2,793	26	0.9	156	1	0.6
Sales workers	5,089	2	*	4,746	2	*	343	—	—
Office and clerical workers	19,603	322	1.6	5,468	163	3.0	14,135	159	1.1
Total white collar	46,323	454	1.0	30,827	291	0.9	15,496	163	1.1
Craftsmen	46,417	2,811	6.1	41,467	2,549	6.1	4,950	262	5.3
Operatives	103,965	13,166	12.7	86,291	11,125	12.9	17,674	2,041	11.5
Laborers	58,006	12,440	21.4	45,380	9,877	21.8	12,626	2,563	20.3
Service workers	3,858	936	24.3	3,546	832	23.5	312	104	33.3
Total blue collar	212,246	29,353	13.8	176,684	24,383	13.8	35,562	4,970	14.0
Total	258,569	29,807	11.5	207,511	24,674	11.9	51,058	5,133	10.1

Source: U.S. Equal Employment Opportunity Commission, *Job Patterns for Minorities and Women in Private Industry, 1966*, Report No. 1 (Washington: The Commission, 1968), Part II.

Note: Sum of regional totals is less than United States total because EEOC did not publish data for those states with fewer than ten reporting establishments unless the state had at least five establishments with at least 2,000 employees.

* Less than 0.05 percent.

TABLE A-3. *Furniture Industry*
Employment by Race, Sex, and Occupational Group
1,092 Establishments, United States, 1967

Occupational Group	All Employees			Male			Female		
	Total	Negro	Percent Negro	Total	Negro	Percent Negro	Total	Negro	Percent Negro
Officials and managers	16,510	120	0.7	15,975	117	0.7	535	3	0.6
Professionals	2,436	17	0.7	2,273	16	0.7	163	1	0.6
Technicians	3,231	40	1.2	3,062	38	1.2	169	2	1.2
Sales workers	5,273	3	0.1	4,909	3	0.1	364	—	—
Office and clerical workers	20,074	411	2.0	5,361	212	4.0	14,713	199	1.4
Total white collar	47,524	591	1.2	31,580	386	1.2	15,944	205	1.3
Craftsmen	49,642	3,492	7.0	44,638	3,167	7.1	5,004	325	6.5
Operatives	113,127	15,715	13.9	89,575	12,727	14.2	23,552	2,988	12.7
Laborers	63,570	14,490	22.8	46,393	10,576	22.8	17,177	3,914	22.8
Service workers	4,224	1,023	24.2	3,861	919	23.8	363	104	28.7
Total blue collar	230,563	34,720	15.1	184,467	27,389	14.8	46,096	7,331	15.9
Total	278,087	35,311	12.7	216,047	27,775	12.9	62,040	7,536	12.1

Source: U.S. Equal Employment Opportunity Commission, *Job Patterns for Minorities and Women in Private Industry, 1967*, Report No. 2 (Washington: The Commission, 1970), Vol. I.

Note: Sum of regional totals is less than United States total because EEOC did not publish data for those states with fewer than ten reporting establishments unless the state had at least five establishments with at least 2,000 employees.

TABLE A-4. *Furniture Industry*
Employment by Race, Sex, and Occupational Group
1,139 Establishments, United States, 1969

Occupational Group	All Employees			Male			Female		
	Total	Negro	Percent Negro	Total	Negro	Percent Negro	Total	Negro	Percent Negro
Officials and managers	17,925	203	1.1	17,329	193	1.1	596	10	1.7
Professionals	2,894	14	0.5	2,689	11	0.4	205	3	1.5
Technicians	3,810	57	1.5	3,523	53	1.5	287	4	1.4
Sales workers	5,802	16	0.3	5,356	9	0.2	446	7	1.6
Office and clerical workers	20,480	509	2.5	5,029	205	4.1	15,451	304	2.0
Total white collar	50,911	799	1.6	33,926	471	1.4	16,985	328	1.9
Craftsmen	48,205	4,271	8.9	42,428	3,664	8.6	5,777	607	10.5
Operatives	107,853	16,944	15.7	82,305	12,834	15.6	25,548	4,110	16.1
Laborers	66,534	14,225	21.4	44,801	10,075	22.5	21,733	4,150	19.1
Service workers	4,393	1,079	24.6	3,868	909	23.5	525	170	32.4
Total blue collar	226,985	36,519	16.1	173,402	27,482	15.8	53,583	9,037	16.9
Total	277,896	37,318	13.4	207,328	27,953	13.5	70,568	9,365	13.3

Source: U.S. Equal Employment Opportunity Commission, 1969.

Note: Sum of regional totals is less than United States total because EEOC did not publish data for those states with fewer than ten reporting establishments unless the state had at least five establishments with at least 2,000 employees.

TABLE A-5. *Furniture Industry*
Employment by Race, Sex, and Occupational Group
1,170 Establishments, United States, 1970

Occupational Group	All Employees			Male			Female		
	Total	Negro	Percent Negro	Total	Negro	Percent Negro	Total	Negro	Percent Negro
Officials and managers	18,652	263	1.4	17,987	247	1.4	665	16	2.4
Professionals	3,150	21	0.7	2,897	17	0.6	253	4	1.6
Technicians	4,147	67	1.6	3,843	61	1.6	304	6	2.0
Sales workers	5,511	17	0.3	5,087	9	0.2	424	8	1.9
Office and clerical workers	19,905	506	2.5	4,562	193	4.2	15,343	313	2.0
Total white collar	51,365	874	1.7	34,376	527	1.5	16,989	347	2.0
Craftsmen	48,060	4,292	8.9	41,551	3,553	8.6	6,509	739	11.4
Operatives	106,895	16,614	15.5	79,397	12,169	15.3	27,498	4,445	16.2
Laborers	59,306	12,908	21.8	38,391	8,629	22.5	20,915	4,279	20.5
Service workers	4,200	968	23.0	3,729	819	22.0	471	149	31.6
Total blue collar	218,461	34,782	15.9	163,068	25,170	15.4	55,393	9,612	17.4
Total	269,826	35,656	13.2	197,444	25,697	13.0	72,382	9,959	13.8

Source: U.S. Equal Employment Opportunity Commission, 1970.

TABLE A-6. *Furniture Industry*
Employment by Race, Sex, and Occupational Group
7 Establishments, New England, 1964

Occupational Group	All Employees			Male			Female		
	Total	Negro	Percent Negro	Total	Negro	Percent Negro	Total	Negro	Percent Negro
Officials and managers	64	—	—	64	—	—	—	—	—
Professionals	9	—	—	8	—	—	1	—	—
Technicians	26	—	—	24	—	—	2	—	—
Sales workers	70	—	—	70	—	—	—	—	—
Office and clerical workers	152	1	0.7	57	1	1.8	95	—	—
Total white collar	321	1	0.3	223	1	0.4	98	—	—
Craftsmen	368	5	1.4	354	5	1.4	14	—	—
Operatives	504	24	4.8	439	19	4.3	65	5	7.7
Laborers	98	4	4.1	94	4	4.3	4	—	—
Service workers	12	—	—	10	—	—	2	—	—
Total blue collar	982	33	3.4	897	28	3.1	85	5	5.9
Total	1,303	34	2.6	1,120	29	2.6	183	5	2.7

Source: Data in author's possession.

TABLE A-7. *Furniture Industry*
Employment by Race, Sex, and Occupational Group
21 Establishments, New England, 1966

Occupational Group	All Employees			Male			Female		
	Total	Negro	Percent Negro	Total	Negro	Percent Negro	Total	Negro	Percent Negro
Officials and managers	245	—	—	240	—	—	5	—	—
Professionals	21	—	—	21	—	—	—	—	—
Technicians	24	—	—	22	—	—	2	—	—
Sales workers	125	1	0.8	118	1	0.8	7	—	—
Office and clerical workers	364	—	—	80	—	—	284	—	—
Total white collar	779	1	0.1	481	1	0.2	298	—	—
Craftsmen	476	2	0.4	401	2	0.5	75	—	—
Operatives	1,670	18	1.1	1,454	17	1.2	216	1	0.5
Laborers	861	26	3.0	611	20	3.3	250	6	2.4
Service workers	32	—	—	31	—	—	1	—	—
Total blue collar	3,039	46	1.5	2,497	39	1.6	542	7	1.3
Total	3,818	47	1.2	2,978	40	1.3	840	7	0.8

Source: U.S. Equal Employment Opportunity Commission, *Job Patterns for Minorities and Women in Private Industry, 1966*, Report No. 1 (Washington: The Commission, 1968), Part II.

TABLE A-8. *Furniture Industry*
Employment by Race, Sex, and Occupational Group
24 Establishments, New England, 1967

Occupational Group	All Employees			Male			Female		
	Total	Negro	Percent Negro	Total	Negro	Percent Negro	Total	Negro	Percent Negro
Officials and managers	206	1	0.5	204	1	0.5	2	—	—
Professionals	20	—	—	19	—	—	1	—	—
Technicians	38	—	—	38	—	—	—	—	—
Sales workers	90	—	—	66	—	—	24	—	—
Office and clerical workers	244	6	2.5	46	—	—	198	6	3.0
Total white collar	598	7	1.2	373	1	0.3	225	6	2.7
Craftsmen	770	18	2.3	700	17	2.4	70	1	1.4
Operatives	1,408	31	2.2	1,045	21	2.0	363	10	2.8
Laborers	650	18	2.8	488	14	2.9	162	4	2.5
Service workers	28	2	7.1	28	2	7.1	—	—	—
Total blue collar	2,856	69	2.4	2,261	54	2.4	595	15	2.5
Total	3,454	76	2.2	2,634	55	2.1	820	21	2.6

Source: U.S. Equal Employment Opportunity Commission, *Job Patterns for Minorities and Women in Private Industry, 1967*, Report No. 2 (Washington: The Commission, 1970), Vol. 1.

TABLE A-9. *Furniture Industry*
Employment by Race, Sex, and Occupational Group
46 Establishments, New England, 1969

Occupational Group	All Employees			Male			Female		
	Total	Negro	Percent Negro	Total	Negro	Percent Negro	Total	Negro	Percent Negro
Officials and managers	477	1	0.2	463	1	0.2	14	—	—
Professionals	83	—	—	78	—	—	5	—	—
Technicians	98	1	1.0	94	1	1.1	4	—	—
Sales workers	153	—	—	129	—	—	24	—	—
Office and clerical workers	655	3	0.5	126	—	—	529	3	0.6
Total white collar	1,466	5	0.3	890	2	0.2	576	3	0.5
Craftsmen	1,607	15	0.9	1,439	14	1.0	168	1	0.6
Operatives	2,614	23	0.9	1,924	13	0.7	690	10	1.4
Laborers	2,186	44	2.0	1,564	25	1.6	622	19	3.1
Service workers	124	1	0.8	111	—	—	13	1	7.7
Total blue collar	6,531	83	1.3	5,038	52	1.0	1,493	31	2.1
Total	7,997	88	1.1	5,928	54	0.9	2,069	34	1.6

Source: U.S. Equal Employment Opportunity Commission, 1969.

TABLE A-10. *Furniture Industry*
Employment by Race, Sex, and Occupational Group
25 Establishments, Middle Atlantic States, 1964

Occupational Group	All Employees			Male			Female		
	Total	Negro	Percent Negro	Total	Negro	Percent Negro	Total	Negro	Percent Negro
Officials and managers	571	3	0.5	557	3	0.5	14	—	—
Professionals	91	1	1.1	83	1	1.2	8	—	—
Technicians	198	—	—	182	—	—	16	—	—
Sales workers	216	—	—	216	—	—	—	—	—
Office and clerical workers	1,050	30	2.9	306	9	2.9	744	21	2.8
Total white collar	2,126	34	1.6	1,344	13	1.0	782	21	2.7
Craftsmen	1,511	84	5.6	1,393	70	5.0	118	14	11.9
Operatives	3,936	329	8.4	3,390	264	7.8	546	65	11.9
Laborers	1,485	101	6.8	1,153	100	8.7	332	1	0.3
Service workers	147	18	12.2	133	15	11.3	14	3	21.4
Total blue collar	7,079	532	7.5	6,069	449	7.4	1,010	83	8.2
Total	9,205	566	6.1	7,413	462	6.2	1,792	104	5.8

Source: Data in author's possession.

TABLE A-11. *Furniture Industry*
Employment by Race, Sex, and Occupational Group
117 Establishments, Middle Atlantic States, 1966

Occupational Group	All Employees			Male			Female		
	Total	Negro	Percent Negro	Total	Negro	Percent Negro	Total	Negro	Percent Negro
Officials and managers	2,341	21	0.9	2,273	20	0.9	68	1	1.5
Professionals	1,185	13	1.1	1,137	13	1.1	48	—	—
Technicians	352	3	0.9	334	3	0.9	18	—	—
Sales workers	776	—	—	721	—	—	55	—	—
Office and clerical workers	3,516	102	2.9	1,006	33	3.3	2,510	69	2.7
Total white collar	8,170	139	1.7	5,471	69	1.3	2,699	70	2.6
Craftsmen	5,441	187	3.4	4,979	158	3.2	462	29	6.3
Operatives	14,687	1,337	9.1	12,228	1,444	9.4	2,459	193	7.8
Laborers	5,388	652	12.1	4,229	504	11.9	1,159	148	12.8
Service workers	543	47	8.7	501	43	8.6	42	4	9.5
Total blue collar	26,059	2,223	8.5	21,937	1,849	8.4	4,122	374	9.1
Total	34,229	2,362	6.9	27,408	1,918	7.0	6,821	444	6.5

Source: U.S. Equal Employment Opportunity Commission, *Job Patterns for Minorities and Women in Private Industry, 1966*, Report No. 1 (Washington: The Commission, 1968), Part II.

TABLE A-12. *Furniture Industry*
Employment by Race, Sex, and Occupational Group
147 Establishments, Middle Atlantic States, 1967

Occupational Group	All Employees			Male			Female		
	Total	Negro	Percent Negro	Total	Negro	Percent Negro	Total	Negro	Percent Negro
Officials and managers	2,300	22	1.0	2,231	21	0.9	69	1	1.4
Professionals	323	5	1.5	296	5	1.7	27	—	—
Technicians	517	6	1.2	489	6	1.2	28	—	—
Sales workers	853	1	0.1	789	1	0.1	64	—	—
Office and clerical workers	3,123	106	3.4	870	41	4.7	2,253	65	2.9
Total white collar	7,116	140	2.0	4,675	74	1.6	2,441	66	2.7
Craftsmen	6,186	261	4.2	5,746	221	3.8	440	40	9.1
Operatives	15,098	1,634	10.8	12,267	1,379	11.2	2,831	255	9.0
Laborers	6,884	964	14.0	5,607	871	15.5	1,277	93	7.3
Service workers	554	43	7.8	518	42	8.1	36	1	2.8
Total blue collar	28,722	2,902	10.1	24,138	2,513	10.4	4,584	389	8.5
Total	35,838	3,042	8.5	28,813	2,587	9.0	7,025	455	6.5

Source: U.S. Equal Employment Opportunity Commission, *Job Patterns for Minorities and Women in Private Industry, 1967*, Report No. 2 (Washington: The Commission, 1970), Vol. I.

TABLE A-13. *Furniture Industry*
Employment by Race, Sex, and Occupational Group
167 Establishments, Middle Atlantic States, 1969

Occupational Group	All Employees			Male			Female		
	Total	Negro	Percent Negro	Total	Negro	Percent Negro	Total	Negro	Percent Negro
Officials and managers	2,512	43	1.7	2,410	38	1.6	102	5	4.9
Professionals	359	6	1.7	334	4	1.2	25	2	8.0
Technicians	607	13	2.1	558	12	2.2	49	1	2.0
Sales workers	1,071	4	0.4	979	2	0.2	92	2	2.2
Office and clerical workers	3,340	194	5.8	912	55	6.0	2,428	139	5.7
Total white collar	7,889	260	3.3	5,193	111	2.1	2,696	149	5.5
Craftsmen	6,396	591	9.2	5,783	524	9.1	613	67	10.9
Operatives	14,595	1,863	12.8	11,624	1,408	12.1	2,971	455	15.3
Laborers	6,864	1,016	14.8	5,399	922	17.1	1,465	94	6.4
Service workers	618	44	7.1	567	41	7.2	51	3	5.9
Total blue collar	28,473	3,514	12.3	23,373	2,895	12.4	5,100	619	12.1
Total	36,362	3,774	10.4	28,566	3,006	10.5	7,796	768	9.9

Source: U.S. Equal Employment Opportunity Commission, 1969.

TABLE A-14. *Furniture Industry*
Employment by Race, Sex, and Occupational Group
162 Establishments, Middle Atlantic States, 1970

Occupational Group	All Employees			Male			Female		
	Total	Negro	Percent Negro	Total	Negro	Percent Negro	Total	Negro	Percent Negro
Officials and managers	2,498	47	1.9	2,395	43	1.8	103	4	3.9
Professionals	423	7	1.7	389	6	1.5	34	1	2.9
Technicians	595	17	2.9	546	17	3.1	49	—	—
Sales workers	862	4	0.5	793	2	0.3	69	2	2.9
Office and clerical workers	2,845	163	5.7	677	34	5.0	2,168	129	6.0
Total white collar	7,223	238	3.3	4,800	102	2.1	2,423	136	5.6
Craftsmen	5,465	345	6.3	4,920	308	6.3	545	37	6.8
Operatives	13,435	1,203	9.0	10,188	993	9.7	3,247	210	6.5
Laborers	6,774	786	11.6	5,004	611	12.2	1,770	175	9.9
Service workers	510	57	11.2	469	55	11.7	41	2	4.9
Total blue collar	26,184	2,391	9.1	20,581	1,967	9.6	5,603	424	7.6
Total	33,407	2,629	7.9	25,381	2,069	8.2	8,026	560	7.0

Source: U.S. Equal Employment Opportunity Commission, 1970.

TABLE A-15. *Furniture Industry*
Employment by Race, Sex, and Occupational Group
25 Establishments, South, 1964

Occupational Group	All Employees			Male			Female		
	Total	Negro	Percent Negro	Total	Negro	Percent Negro	Total	Negro	Percent Negro
Officials and managers	316	1	0.3	309	1	0.3	7	—	—
Professionals	253	—	—	249	—	—	4	—	—
Technicians	232	—	—	226	—	—	6	—	—
Sales workers	356	—	—	350	—	—	6	—	—
Office and clerical workers	782	8	1.0	206	6	2.9	576	2	0.3
Total white collar	1,939	9	0.5	1,340	7	0.5	599	2	0.3
Craftsmen	1,320	37	2.8	1,242	37	3.0	78	—	—
Operatives	3,751	441	11.8	3,335	416	12.5	416	25	6.0
Laborers	5,634	329	5.8	4,919	309	6.3	715	20	2.8
Service workers	249	77	30.9	238	69	29.0	11	8	72.7
Total blue collar	10,954	884	8.1	9,734	831	8.5	1,220	53	4.3
Total	12,893	893	6.9	11,074	838	7.6	1,819	55	3.0

Source: Data in another's possession.

TABLE A-16. *Furniture Industry*
Employment by Race, Sex, and Occupational Group
447 Establishments, South, 1966

Occupational Group	All Employees			Male			Female		
	Total	Negro	Percent Negro	Total	Negro	Percent Negro	Total	Negro	Percent Negro
Officials and managers	6,085	26	0.4	5,878	25	0.4	207	1	0.5
Professionals	706	1	0.1	667	1	0.1	39	—	—
Technicians	862	1	0.1	798	1	0.1	64	—	—
Sales workers	1,593	1	0.1	1,515	1	0.1	78	—	—
Office and clerical workers	7,069	108	1.5	1,812	77	4.2	5,257	31	0.6
Total white collar	16,315	137	0.8	10,670	105	1.0	5,645	32	0.6
Craftsmen	25,070	1,916	7.6	22,659	1,790	7.9	2,411	126	5.2
Operatives	49,224	8,187	16.6	41,755	6,911	16.6	7,469	1,276	17.1
Laborers	31,723	9,130	28.8	25,311	7,456	29.5	6,412	1,674	26.1
Service workers	1,912	760	39.7	1,747	673	38.5	165	87	52.7
Total blue collar	107,929	19,993	18.5	91,472	16,830	18.4	16,457	3,163	19.2
Total	124,244	20,130	16.2	102,142	16,935	16.6	22,102	3,195	14.5

Source: U.S. Equal Employment Opportunity Commission, *Job Patterns for Minorities and Women in Private Industry, 1966*, Report No. 1 (Washington: The Commission, 1968), Part II.

TABLE A-17. *Furniture Industry*
Employment by Race, Sex, and Occupational Group
492 Establishments, South, 1967

Occupational Group	All Employees			Male			Female		
	Total	Negro	Percent Negro	Total	Negro	Percent Negro	Total	Negro	Percent Negro
Officials and managers	7,377	47	0.6	7,162	46	0.6	215	1	0.5
Professionals	856	2	0.2	791	1	0.1	65	1	1.5
Technicians	1,034	13	1.3	959	13	1.4	75	—	—
Sales workers	1,659	2	0.1	1,580	2	0.1	79	—	—
Office and clerical workers	7,818	139	1.8	2,005	103	5.1	5,813	36	0.6
Total white collar	18,744	203	1.1	12,497	165	1.3	6,247	38	0.6
Craftsmen	26,976	2,162	8.0	24,245	2,007	8.3	2,731	155	5.7
Operatives	55,994	10,678	19.1	44,885	8,563	19.1	11,109	2,115	19.0
Laborers	36,221	11,419	31.5	26,144	8,067	30.9	10,077	3,352	33.3
Service workers	2,172	811	37.3	2,010	728	36.2	162	83	51.2
Total blue collar	121,363	25,070	20.7	97,284	19,365	19.9	24,079	5,705	23.7
Total	140,107	25,273	18.0	109,781	19,530	17.8	30,326	5,743	18.9

Source: U.S. Equal Employment Opportunity Commission, *Job Patterns for Minorities and Women in Private Industry, 1967*, Report No. 2 (Washington: The Commission, 1970), Vol. I.

TABLE A-18. *Furniture Industry*
Employment by Race, Sex, and Occupational Group
504 Establishments, South, 1969

Occupational Group	All Employees			Male			Female		
	Total	Negro	Percent Negro	Total	Negro	Percent Negro	Total	Negro	Percent Negro
Officials and managers	8,061	94	1.2	7,792	20	1.2	269	4	1.5
Professionals	933	3	0.3	837	2	0.2	96	1	1.0
Technicians	1,167	16	1.4	1,047	15	1.4	120	1	0.8
Sales workers	1,807	6	0.3	1,684	4	0.2	123	2	1.6
Office and clerical workers	7,718	169	2.2	1,761	100	5.7	5,957	69	1.2
Total white collar	19,686	288	1.5	13,121	211	1.6	6,565	77	1.2
Craftsmen	26,973	2,787	10.3	23,627	2,421	10.2	3,346	366	10.9
Operatives	54,847	12,395	22.6	41,952	9,374	22.3	12,895	3,021	23.4
Laborers	36,341	11,129	30.6	24,142	7,660	31.7	12,199	3,469	28.4
Service workers	2,346	895	38.2	2,109	751	35.6	237	144	60.8
Total blue collar	120,507	27,206	22.6	91,830	20,206	22.0	28,677	7,000	24.4
Total	140,193	27,494	19.6	104,951	20,417	19.5	35,242	7,077	20.1

Source: U.S. Equal Employment Opportunity Commission, 1969.

TABLE A-19. *Furniture Industry*
Employment by Race, Sex, and Occupational Group
521 Establishments, South, 1970

Occupational Group	All Employees			Male			Female		
	Total	Negro	Percent Negro	Total	Negro	Percent Negro	Total	Negro	Percent Negro
Officials and managers	8,410	116	1.4	8,129	113	1.4	281	3	1.1
Professionals	972	4	0.4	887	3	0.3	85	1	1.2
Technicians	1,237	20	1.6	1,125	16	1.4	112	4	3.6
Sales workers	1,688	5	0.3	1,565	3	0.2	123	2	1.6
Office and clerical workers	7,439	183	2.5	1,598	108	6.8	5,841	75	1.3
Total white collar	19,746	328	1.7	13,304	243	1.8	6,442	85	1.3
Craftsmen	27,490	2,890	10.5	23,593	2,416	10.2	3,897	474	12.2
Operatives	54,176	12,452	23.0	39,813	8,881	22.3	14,363	3,571	24.9
Laborers	32,202	10,027	31.1	20,163	6,566	32.6	12,039	3,461	28.7
Service workers	2,296	758	33.0	2,039	640	31.4	257	118	45.9
Total blue collar	116,164	26,127	22.5	85,608	18,503	21.6	30,556	7,624	25.0
Total	135,910	26,455	19.5	98,912	18,746	19.0	36,998	7,709	20.8

Source: U.S. Equal Employment Opportunity Commission, 1970.

TABLE A-20. *Furniture Industry*
Employment by Race, Sex, and Occupational Group
35 Establishments, Midwest, 1964

Occupational Group	All Employees			Male			Female		
	Total	Negro	Percent Negro	Total	Negro	Percent Negro	Total	Negro	Percent Negro
Officials and managers	1,088	4	0.4	1,065	3	0.3	23	1	4.3
Professionals	263	1	0.4	247	1	0.4	16	—	—
Technicians	363	1	0.3	352	1	0.3	11	—	—
Sales workers	692	—	—	663	—	—	29	—	—
Office and clerical workers	1,948	15	0.8	654	10	1.5	1,294	5	0.4
Total white collar	4,354	21	0.5	2,981	15	0.5	1,373	6	0.4
Craftsmen	2,060	90	4.4	1,977	85	4.3	83	5	6.0
Operatives	6,016	503	8.4	4,990	410	8.2	1,026	93	9.1
Laborers	2,271	266	11.7	1,920	193	10.1	351	73	20.8
Service workers	243	45	18.5	206	35	17.0	37	10	27.0
Total blue collar	10,590	904	8.5	9,093	723	8.0	1,497	181	12.1
Total	14,944	925	6.2	12,074	738	6.1	2,870	187	6.5

Source: Data in author's possession.

TABLE A-21. *Furniture Industry*
Employment by Race, Sex, and Occupational Group
251 Establishments, Midwest, 1966

Occupational Group	All Employees			Male			Female		
	Total	Negro	Percent Negro	Total	Negro	Percent Negro	Total	Negro	Percent Negro
Officials and managers	5,314	23	0.4	4,947	22	0.4	367	1	0.3
Professionals	957	6	0.6	899	6	0.7	58	—	—
Technicians	1,330	14	1.1	1,282	13	1.0	48	1	2.1
Sales workers	1,693	—	—	1,571	—	—	122	—	—
Office and clerical workers	6,403	74	1.2	1,909	36	1.9	4,494	38	0.8
Total white collar	15,697	117	0.7	10,608	77	0.7	5,089	40	0.8
Craftsmen	10,765	529	4.9	9,472	446	4.7	1,293	83	6.4
Operatives	28,837	2,798	9.7	23,468	2,333	9.9	5,369	465	8.7
Laborers	13,594	1,421	10.5	10,518	1,205	11.5	3,076	216	7.0
Service workers	1,038	83	8.0	957	74	7.7	81	9	11.1
Total blue collar	54,234	4,831	8.9	44,415	4,058	9.1	9,819	773	7.9
Total	69,931	4,948	7.1	55,023	4,135	7.5	14,908	813	5.5

Source: U.S. Equal Employment Opportunity Commission, *Job Patterns for Minorities and Women in Private Industry, 1966*, Report No. 1 (Washington: The Commission, 1968), Part II.

TABLE A-22. *Furniture Industry*
Employment by Race, Sex, and Occupational Group
272 Establishments, Midwest, 1967

Occupational Group	All Employees			Male			Female		
	Total	Negro	Percent Negro	Total	Negro	Percent Negro	Total	Negro	Percent Negro
Officials and managers	4,857	26	0.5	4,710	25	0.5	147	1	0.7
Professionals	942	3	0.3	894	3	0.3	48	—	—
Technicians	1,354	14	1.0	1,303	13	1.0	51	1	2.0
Sales workers	1,748	—	—	1,656	—	—	92	—	—
Office and clerical workers	6,591	120	1.8	1,773	44	2.5	4,818	76	1.6
Total white collar	15,492	163	1.1	10,336	85	0.8	5,156	78	1.5
Craftsmen	11,533	880	7.6	10,194	769	7.5	1,339	111	8.3
Operatives	30,658	2,404	7.8	23,618	1,892	8.0	7,040	512	7.3
Laborers	13,753	1,519	11.0	9,500	1,150	12.1	4,253	369	8.7
Service workers	1,138	130	11.4	986	114	11.6	152	16	10.5
Total blue collar	57,082	4,933	8.6	44,298	3,925	8.9	12,784	1,008	7.9
Total	72,574	5,096	7.0	54,634	4,010	7.3	17,940	1,086	6.1

Source: U.S. Equal Employment Opportunity Commission, *Job Patterns for Minorities and Women in Private Industry, 1967*, Report No. 2 (Washington: The Commission, 1970), Vol. 1.

TABLE A-23. *Furniture Industry*
Employment by Race, Sex, and Occupational Group
306 Establishments, Midwest, 1969

Occupational Group	All Employees			Male			Female		
	Total	Negro	Percent Negro	Total	Negro	Percent Negro	Total	Negro	Percent Negro
Officials and managers	5,732	49	0.9	5,559	48	0.9	173	1	0.6
Professionals	1,317	3	0.2	1,251	3	0.2	66	—	—
Technicians	1,787	22	1.2	1,688	20	1.2	99	2	2.0
Sales workers	2,200	5	0.2	2,036	2	0.1	164	3	1.8
Office and clerical workers	7,297	124	1.7	1,871	43	2.3	5,426	81	1.5
Total white collar	18,333	203	1.1	12,405	116	0.9	5,928	87	1.5
Craftsmen	10,016	693	6.9	8,745	549	6.3	1,271	144	11.3
Operatives	29,449	2,000	6.8	21,519	1,436	6.7	7,930	564	7.1
Laborers	16,895	1,644	9.7	10,583	1,141	10.8	6,312	503	8.0
Service workers	1,081	111	10.3	902	95	10.5	179	16	8.9
Total blue collar	57,441	4,448	7.7	41,749	3,221	7.7	15,692	1,227	7.8
Total	75,774	4,651	6.1	54,154	3,337	6.2	21,620	1,314	6.1

Source: U.S. Equal Employment Opportunity Commission, 1969.

TABLE A-24. *Furniture Industry*
Employment by Race, Sex, and Occupational Group
262 Establishments, Midwest, 1970

Occupational Group	All Employees			Male			Female		
	Total	Negro	Percent Negro	Total	Negro	Percent Negro	Total	Negro	Percent Negro
Officials and managers	5,203	72	1.4	5,013	63	1.3	190	9	4.7
Professionals	1,347	7	0.5	1,252	7	0.6	95	—	—
Technicians	1,673	17	1.0	1,564	16	1.0	109	1	0.9
Sales workers	1,698	2	0.1	1,583	2	0.1	115	—	—
Office and clerical workers	6,403	107	1.7	1,518	35	2.3	4,885	72	1.5
Total white collar	16,324	205	1.3	10,930	123	1.1	5,394	82	1.5
Craftsmen	8,292	713	8.6	7,245	531	7.3	1,047	182	17.4
Operatives	25,122	1,871	7.4	18,868	1,418	7.5	6,254	453	7.2
Laborers	12,544	1,257	10.0	7,734	783	10.1	4,810	474	9.9
Service workers	964	106	11.0	841	89	10.6	123	17	13.8
Total blue collar	46,922	3,947	8.4	34,688	2,821	8.1	12,234	1,126	9.2
Total	63,246	4,152	6.6	45,618	2,944	6.5	17,628	1,208	6.9

Source: U.S. Equal Employment Opportunity Commission, 1970.

TABLE A-25. *Furniture Industry*
Employment by Race, Sex, and Occupational Group
12 Establishments, West (Pacific), 1964

Occupational Group	All Employees			Male			Female		
	Total	Negro	Percent Negro	Total	Negro	Percent Negro	Total	Negro	Percent Negro
Officials and managers	141	—	—	138	—	—	3	—	—
Professionals	76	—	—	74	—	—	2	—	—
Technicians	30	3	10.0	29	3	10.3	1	—	—
Sales workers	85	—	—	77	—	—	8	—	—
Office and clerical workers	311	4	1.3	102	1	1.0	209	3	1.4
Total white collar	643	7	1.1	420	4	1.0	223	3	1.3
Craftsmen	448	17	3.8	394	15	3.8	54	2	3.7
Operatives	1,647	187	11.4	1,381	152	11.0	266	35	13.2
Laborers	111	6	5.4	102	6	5.9	9	—	—
Service workers	39	16	41.0	31	16	51.6	8	—	—
Total blue collar	2,245	226	10.1	1,908	189	9.9	337	37	11.0
Total	2,888	233	8.1	2,328	193	8.3	560	40	7.1

Source: Data in author's possession.

TABLE A-26. *Furniture Industry*
Employment by Race, Sex, and Occupational Group
57 Establishments, West (Pacific), 1966

Occupational Group	All Employees			Male			Female		
	Total	Negro	Percent Negro	Total	Negro	Percent Negro	Total	Negro	Percent Negro
Officials and managers	575	9	1.6	552	9	1.6	23	—	—
Professionals	130	—	—	118	—	—	12	—	—
Technicians	126	6	4.8	115	6	5.2	11	—	—
Sales workers	347	—	—	309	—	—	38	—	—
Office and clerical workers	911	21	2.3	268	12	4.5	643	9	1.4
Total white collar	2,089	36	1.7	1,362	27	2.0	727	9	1.2
Craftsmen	2,001	133	6.6	1,629	111	6.8	372	22	5.9
Operatives	3,416	378	11.1	2,711	328	12.1	705	50	7.1
Laborers	1,580	346	21.9	1,323	336	25.4	257	10	3.9
Service workers	138	28	20.3	129	28	21.7	9	—	—
Total blue collar	7,135	885	12.4	5,792	803	13.9	1,343	82	6.1
Total	9,224	921	10.0	7,154	830	11.6	2,070	91	4.4

Source: U.S. Equal Employment Opportunity Commission, *Job Patterns for Minorities and Women in Private Industry, 1966,* Report No. 1 (Washington: The Commission, 1968), Part II.

TABLE A-27. *Furniture Industry*
Employment by Race, Sex, and Occupational Group
81 Establishments, West (Pacific), 1967

Occupational Group	All Employees			Male			Female		
	Total	Negro	Percent Negro	Total	Negro	Percent Negro	Total	Negro	Percent Negro
Officials and managers	847	14	1.7	817	14	1.7	30	—	—
Professionals	143	6	4.2	132	6	4.5	11	—	—
Technicians	82	5	6.1	78	4	5.1	4	1	25.0
Sales workers	465	—	—	415	—	—	50	—	—
Office and clerical workers	1,222	29	2.4	382	20	5.2	840	9	1.1
Total white collar	2,759	54	2.0	1,824	44	2.4	935	10	1.1
Craftsmen	2,275	142	6.2	1,947	125	6.4	328	17	5.2
Operatives	5,209	766	14.7	4,202	692	16.5	1,007	74	7.3
Laborers	2,879	281	9.8	2,310	262	11.3	569	19	3.3
Service workers	159	23	14.5	155	22	14.2	4	1	25.0
Total blue collar	10,522	1,212	11.5	8,614	1,101	12.8	1,908	111	5.8
Total	13,281	1,266	9.5	10,438	1,145	11.0	2,843	121	4.3

Source: U.S. Equal Employment Opportunity Commission, *Job Patterns for Minorities and Women in Private Industry, 1967,* Report No. 2 (Washington: The Commission, 1970), Vol. I.

TABLE A-28. *Furniture Industry*
Employment by Race, Sex, and Occupational Group
102 Establishments, West (Pacific), 1969

Occupational Group	All Employees			Male			Female		
	Total	Negro	Percent Negro	Total	Negro	Percent Negro	Total	Negro	Percent Negro
Officials and managers	1,066	16	1.5	1,029	16	1.6	37	—	—
Professionals	198	2	1.0	185	2	1.1	13	—	—
Technicians	134	5	3.7	119	5	4.2	15	—	—
Sales workers	533	1	0.2	490	1	0.2	43	—	—
Official and clerical workers	1,366	18	1.3	330	6	1.8	1,036	12	1.2
Total white collar	3,297	42	1.3	2,153	30	1.4	1,144	12	1.0
Craftsmen	3,000	179	6.0	2,658	150	5.6	342	29	8.5
Operatives	5,905	637	10.8	4,899	578	11.8	1,006	59	5.9
Laborers	3,422	353	10.3	2,546	300	11.8	876	53	6.1
Service workers	173	22	12.7	145	18	12.4	28	4	14.3
Total blue collar	12,500	1,191	9.5	10,248	1,046	10.2	2,252	145	6.4
Total	15,797	1,233	7.8	12,401	1,076	8.7	3,396	157	4.6

Source: U.S. Equal Employment Opportunity Commission, 1969.

TABLE A-29. *Furniture Industry*
Employment by Race, Sex, and Occupational Group
177 Establishments, North Carolina, 1966

Occupational Group	All Employees			Male			Female		
	Total	Negro	Percent Negro	Total	Negro	Percent Negro	Total	Negro	Percent Negro
Officials and managers	2,251	10	0.4	2,140	9	0.4	111	1	0.9
Professionals	245	—	—	232	—	—	13	—	—
Technicians	287	—	—	276	—	—	11	—	—
Sales workers	678	1	0.1	654	1	0.2	24	—	—
Office and clerical workers	2,409	31	1.3	590	18	3.1	1,819	13	0.7
Total white collar	5,870	42	0.7	3,892	28	0.7	1,978	14	0.7
Craftsmen	12,394	680	5.5	11,095	641	5.8	1,299	39	3.0
Operatives	19,040	2,596	13.6	16,160	2,154	13.3	2,880	442	15.3
Laborers	10,832	2,044	18.9	8,798	1,568	17.8	2,034	476	23.4
Service workers	816	307	37.6	751	270	36.0	65	37	56.9
Total blue collar	43,082	5,627	13.1	36,804	4,633	12.6	6,278	994	15.8
Total	48,952	5,669	11.6	40,696	4,661	11.5	8,256	1,008	12.2

Source: U.S. Equal Employment Opportunity Commission, 1966.

TABLE A-30. *Furniture Industry*
Employment by Race, Sex, and Occupational Group
194 Establishments, North Carolina, 1967

Occupational Group	All Employees			Male			Female		
	Total	Negro	Percent Negro	Total	Negro	Percent Negro	Total	Negro	Percent Negro
Officials and managers	2,686	7	0.3	2,580	6	0.2	106	1	0.9
Professionals	314	—	—	284	—	—	30	—	—
Technicians	330	1	0.3	313	1	0.3	17	—	—
Sales workers	639	1	0.2	618	1	0.2	21	—	—
Office and clerical workers	2,642	34	1.3	614	23	3.7	2,028	11	0.5
Total white collar	6,611	43	0.7	4,409	31	0.7	2,202	12	0.5
Craftsmen	13,878	888	6.4	12,253	797	6.5	1,625	91	5.6
Operatives	20,851	3,332	16.0	17,024	2,540	14.9	3,827	792	20.7
Laborers	12,012	2,704	22.5	8,817	1,787	20.3	3,195	917	28.7
Service workers	980	335	34.2	918	307	33.4	62	28	45.2
Total blue collar	47,721	7,259	15.2	39,012	5,431	13.9	8,709	1,828	21.0
Total	54,332	7,302	13.4	43,421	5,462	12.6	10,911	1,840	16.9

Source: U.S. Equal Employment Opportunity Commission, 1967.

TABLE A-31. *Furniture Industry*
Employment by Race, Sex, and Occupational Group
180 Establishments, North Carolina, 1969

Occupational Group	All Employees			Male			Female		
	Total	Negro	Percent Negro	Total	Negro	Percent Negro	Total	Negro	Percent Negro
Officials and managers	2,751	21	0.8	2,633	19	0.7	118	2	1.7
Professionals	315	—	—	284	—	—	31	—	—
Technicians	406	4	1.0	334	4	1.2	72	—	—
Sales workers	634	3	0.5	621	2	0.3	13	1	7.7
Office and clerical workers	2,727	54	2.0	612	24	3.9	2,115	30	1.4
Total white collar	6,833	82	1.2	4,484	49	1.1	2,349	33	1.4
Craftsmen	14,464	1,074	7.4	12,253	860	7.0	2,210	214	9.7
Operatives	19,975	3,677	18.4	15,407	2,569	16.7	4,568	1,108	24.3
Laborers	11,684	2,927	25.1	7,713	1,802	23.4	3,971	1,125	28.3
Service workers	1,158	387	33.4	1,013	305	30.1	145	82	56.6
Total blue collar	47,280	8,065	17.1	36,386	5,536	15.2	10,894	2,529	23.2
Total	54,113	8,147	15.1	40,870	5,585	13.7	13,243	2,562	19.3

Source: U.S. Equal Employment Opportunity Commission, 1969.

TABLE A-32. Furniture Industry
Employment by Race, Sex, and Occupational Group
211 Establishments, North Carolina, 1970

Occupational Group	All Employees			Male			Female		
	Total	Negro	Percent Negro	Total	Negro	Percent Negro	Total	Negro	Percent Negro
Officials and managers	3,186	13	1.0	3,061	31	1.0	125	—	—
Professionals	338	—	—	306	—	—	32	—	—
Technicians	480	3	0.6	423	3	0.7	57	—	—
Sales workers	647	1	0.2	598	—	—	49	1	2.0
Office and clerical workers	2,754	86	3.1	581	56	9.6	2,173	30	1.4
Total white collar	7,405	121	1.6	4,969	90	1.8	2,436	31	1.3
Craftsmen	15,099	1,218	8.1	12,555	953	7.6	2,544	265	10.4
Operatives	19,436	3,422	17.6	14,170	2,296	16.2	5,266	1,126	21.4
Laborers	10,602	2,639	24.9	6,433	1,461	22.7	4,169	1,178	28.3
Service workers	1,036	313	30.2	896	259	28.9	140	54	38.6
Total blue collar	46,173	7,592	16.4	34,054	4,969	14.6	12,119	2,623	21.6
Total	53,578	7,713	14.4	39,023	5,059	13.0	14,555	2,654	18.2

Source: U.S. Equal Employment Opportunity Commission, 1970.

TABLE A-33. *Furniture Industry*
Employment by Race, Sex, and Occupational Group
57 Establishments, California, 1966

Occupational Group	All Employees			Male			Female		
	Total	Negro	Percent Negro	Total	Negro	Percent Negro	Total	Negro	Percent Negro
Officials and managers	575	9	1.6	552	9	1.6	23	—	—
Professionals	130	—	—	118	—	—	12	—	—
Technicians	126	6	4.8	115	6	5.2	11	—	—
Sales workers	347	—	—	309	—	—	38	—	—
Office and clerical workers	911	21	2.3	268	12	4.5	643	9	1.4
Total white collar	2,089	36	1.7	1,362	27	2.0	727	9	1.2
Craftsmen	2,001	133	6.6	1,629	111	6.8	372	22	5.9
Operatives	3,416	378	11.1	2,711	328	12.1	705	50	7.1
Laborers	1,580	346	21.9	1,323	336	25.4	257	10	3.9
Service workers	138	28	20.3	129	28	21.7	9	—	—
Total blue collar	7,135	885	12.4	5,792	803	13.9	1,343	82	6.1
Total	9,224	921	10.0	7,154	830	11.6	2,070	91	4.4

Source: U.S. Equal Employment Opportunity Commission, 1966.

TABLE A-34. *Furniture Industry*
Employment by Race, Sex, and Occupational Group
71 Establishments, California, 1967

Occupational Group	All Employees			Male			Female		
	Total	Negro	Percent Negro	Total	Negro	Percent Negro	Total	Negro	Percent Negro
Officials and managers	729	14	1.9	704	14	2.0	25	—	—
Professionals	138	6	4.3	128	6	4.7	10	—	—
Technicians	79	5	6.3	75	4	5.3	4	1	25.0
Sales workers	395	—	—	356	—	—	39	—	—
Office and clerical workers	1,115	29	2.6	354	20	5.6	761	9	1.2
Total white collar	2,456	54	2.2	1,617	44	2.7	839	10	1.2
Craftsmen	1,933	140	7.2	1,640	123	7.5	293	17	5.8
Operatives	4,574	753	16.5	3,669	680	18.5	905	73	8.1
Laborers	2,147	274	12.8	1,768	256	14.5	379	18	4.7
Service workers	156	23	14.7	153	22	14.4	3	1	33.3
Total blue collar	8,810	1,190	13.5	7,230	1,081	15.0	1,580	109	6.9
Total	11,266	1,244	11.0	8,847	1,125	12.7	2,419	119	4.9

Source: U.S. Equal Employment Opportunity Commission, 1967.

TABLE A-35. *Furniture Industry*
Employment by Race, Sex, and Occupational Group
81 Establishments, California, 1969

Occupational Group	All Employees			Male			Female		
	Total	Negro	Percent Negro	Total	Negro	Percent Negro	Total	Negro	Percent Negro
Officials and managers	859	16	1.9	830	16	1.9	29	—	—
Professionals	175	2	1.1	163	2	1.2	12	—	—
Technicians	112	5	4.5	98	5	5.1	14	—	—
Sales workers	425	1	0.2	388	1	0.3	37	—	—
Office and clerical workers	1,154	17	1.5	295	6	2.0	859	11	1.3
Total white collar	2,725	41	1.5	1,774	30	1.7	951	11	1.2
Craftsmen	2,418	170	7.0	2,143	141	6.6	275	29	10.5
Operatives	4,910	623	12.7	4,083	564	13.8	827	59	7.1
Laborers	2,077	343	16.5	1,725	293	17.0	352	50	14.2
Service workers	163	21	12.9	137	18	13.1	26	3	11.5
Total blue collar	9,568	1,157	12.1	8,088	1,016	12.6	1,480	141	9.5
Total	12,293	1,198	9.7	9,862	1,046	10.6	2,431	152	6.3

Source: U.S. Equal Employment Opportunity Commission, 1969.

TABLE A-36. *Furniture Industry*
Employment by Race, Sex, and Occupational Group
84 Establishments, California, 1970

Occupational Group	All Employees			Male			Female		
	Total	Negro	Percent Negro	Total	Negro	Percent Negro	Total	Negro	Percent Negro
Officials and managers	895	19	2.1	854	19	2.2	41	—	—
Professionals	126	2	1.6	113	1	0.9	13	1	7.7
Technicians	126	7	5.6	117	6	5.1	9	1	11.1
Sales workers	463	1	0.2	424	1	0.2	39	—	—
Office and clerical workers	1,089	22	2.0	263	6	2.3	826	16	1.9
Total white collar	2,699	51	1.9	1,771	33	1.9	928	18	1.9
Craftsmen	2,477	184	7.4	2,183	145	6.6	294	39	13.3
Operatives	4,761	574	12.1	3,742	481	12.9	1,019	93	9.1
Laborers	2,214	267	12.1	1,794	246	13.7	420	21	5.0
Service workers	101	11	10.9	95	9	9.5	6	2	33.3
Total blue collar	9,553	1,036	10.8	7,814	881	11.3	1,739	155	8.9
Total	12,252	1,087	8.9	9,585	914	9.5	2,667	173	6.5

Source: U.S. Equal Employment Opportunity Commission, 1970.

TABLE A-37. *Furniture Industry*
Employment by Race, Sex, and Occupational Group
48 Establishments, New York, 1966

Occupational Group	All Employees			Male			Female		
	Total	Negro	Percent Negro	Total	Negro	Percent Negro	Total	Negro	Percent Negro
Officials and managers	963	8	0.8	932	8	0.9	31	—	—
Professionals	103	1	1.0	92	1	1.1	11	—	—
Technicians	177	2	1.1	167	2	1.2	10	—	—
Sales workers	434	—	—	408	—	—	26	—	—
Office and clerical workers	1,345	39	2.9	313	13	4.2	1,032	26	2.5
Total white collar	3,022	50	1.7	1,912	24	1.3	1,110	26	2.3
Craftsmen	2,453	51	2.1	2,217	42	1.9	236	9	3.8
Operatives	5,698	170	3.0	4,790	140	2.9	908	30	3.3
Laborers	1,790	236	13.2	1,537	220	14.3	253	16	6.3
Service workers	249	21	8.4	229	18	7.9	20	3	15.0
Total blue collar	10,190	478	4.7	8,773	420	4.8	1,417	58	4.1
Total	13,212	528	4.0	10,685	444	4.2	2,527	84	3.3

Source: U.S. Equal Employment Opportunity Commission, 1966.

TABLE A-38. *Furniture Industry*
Employment by Race, Sex, and Occupational Group
62 Establishments, New York, 1967

Occupational Group	All Employees			Male			Female		
	Total	Negro	Percent Negro	Total	Negro	Percent Negro	Total	Negro	Percent Negro
Officials and managers	1,096	9	0.8	1,057	9	0.9	39	—	—
Professionals	156	3	1.9	137	3	2.2	19	—	—
Technicians	261	5	1.9	245	5	2.0	16	—	—
Sales workers	502	—	—	467	—	—	35	—	—
Office and clerical workers	1,560	42	2.7	386	15	3.9	1,174	27	2.3
Total white collar	3,575	59	1.7	2,292	32	1.4	1,283	27	2.1
Craftsmen	2,969	75	2.5	2,723	60	2.2	246	15	6.1
Operatives	6,320	360	5.7	5,075	301	5.9	1,245	59	4.7
Laborers	2,872	400	13.9	2,361	355	15.0	511	45	8.8
Service workers	291	21	7.2	264	21	8.0	27	—	—
Total blue collar	12,452	856	6.9	10,423	737	7.1	2,029	119	5.9
Total	16,027	915	5.7	12,715	769	6.0	3,312	146	4.4

Source: U.S. Equal Employment Opportunity Commission, 1967.

TABLE A-39. *Furniture Industry*

Employment by Race, Sex, and Occupational Group

63 Establishments, New York, 1969

Occupational Group	All Employees			Male			Female		
	Total	Negro	Percent Negro	Total	Negro	Percent Negro	Total	Negro	Percent Negro
Officials and managers	952	13	1.4	908	11	1.2	44	2	4.5
Professionals	149	3	2.0	137	2	1.5	12	1	8.3
Technicians	207	5	2.4	184	4	2.2	23	1	4.3
Sales workers	614	—	—	575	—	—	39	—	—
Office and clerical workers	1,264	70	5.5	293	11	3.8	971	59	6.1
Total white collar	3,186	91	2.9	2,097	28	1.3	1,089	63	5.8
Craftsmen	2,238	107	4.8	1,981	97	4.9	257	10	3.9
Operatives	4,548	349	7.7	3,518	282	8.0	1,030	67	6.5
Laborers	2,673	362	13.5	1,980	322	16.3	693	40	5.8
Service workers	181	24	13.3	162	21	13.0	19	3	15.8
Total blue collar	9,640	842	8.7	7,641	722	9.4	1,999	120	6.0
Total	12,826	933	7.3	9,738	750	7.7	3,088	183	5.9

Source: U.S. Equal Employment Opportunity Commission, 1969.

TABLE A-40. *Furniture Industry*
Employment by Race, Sex, and Occupational Group
66 Establishments, New York, 1970

Occupational Group	All Employees			Male			Female		
	Total	Negro	Percent Negro	Total	Negro	Percent Negro	Total	Negro	Percent Negro
Officials and managers	1,022	20	2.0	973	18	1.8	49	2	4.1
Professionals	192	3	1.6	168	3	1.8	24	—	—
Technicians	251	6	2.4	228	6	2.6	23	—	—
Sales workers	456	1	0.2	431	—	—	25	1	4.0
Office and clerical workers	1,363	83	6.1	321	16	5.0	1,042	67	6.4
Total white collar	3,284	113	3.4	2,121	43	2.0	1,163	70	6.0
Craftsmen	2,174	149	6.9	1,918	127	6.6	256	22	8.6
Operatives	5,060	359	7.1	3,958	321	8.1	1,102	38	3.4
Laborers	2,492	373	15.0	1,802	253	14.0	690	120	17.4
Service workers	197	24	12.2	176	23	13.1	21	1	4.8
Total blue collar	9,923	905	9.1	7,854	724	9.2	2,069	181	8.7
Total	13,207	1,018	7.7	9,975	767	7.7	3,232	251	7.8

Source: U.S. Equal Employment Opportunity Commission, 1970.

TABLE A-41. *Furniture Industry*
Employment by Race, Sex, and Occupational Group
57 Establishments, Pennsylvania, 1966

Occupational Group	All Employees			Male			Female		
	Total	Negro	Percent Negro	Total	Negro	Percent Negro	Total	Negro	Percent Negro
Officials and managers	1,052	5	0.5	1,031	5	0.5	21	—	—
Professionals	1,042	12	1.2	1,006	12	1.2	36	—	—
Technicians	155	1	0.6	149	1	0.7	6	—	—
Sales workers	186	—	—	175	—	—	11	—	—
Office and clerical workers	1,327	18	1.4	528	12	2.3	799	6	0.8
Total white collar	3,762	36	1.0	2,889	30	1.0	873	6	0.7
Craftsmen	2,481	49	2.0	2,344	49	2.1	137	—	—
Operatives	6,962	567	8.1	5,819	493	8.5	1,143	74	6.5
Laborers	2,539	160	6.3	1,979	138	7.0	560	22	3.9
Service workers	230	15	6.5	212	14	6.6	18	1	5.6
Total blue collar	12,212	791	6.5	10,354	694	6.7	1,858	97	5.2
Total	15,974	827	5.2	13,243	724	5.5	2,731	103	3.8

Source: U.S. Equal Employment Opportunity Commission, 1966.

TABLE A-42. *Furniture Industry*
Employment by Race, Sex, and Occupational Group
72 Establishments, Pennsylvania, 1967

Occupational Group	All Employees			Male			Female		
	Total	Negro	Percent Negro	Total	Negro	Percent Negro	Total	Negro	Percent Negro
Officials and managers	938	—	—	920	—	—	18	—	—
Professionals	95	—	—	88	—	—	7	—	—
Technicians	185	—	—	183	—	—	2	—	—
Sales workers	208	—	—	192	—	—	16	—	—
Office and clerical workers	1,037	7	0.7	316	5	1.6	721	2	0.3
Total white collar	2,463	7	0.3	1,699	5	0.3	764	2	0.3
Craftsmen	2,573	28	1.1	2,465	28	1.1	108	—	—
Operatives	6,691	610	9.1	5,527	583	10.5	1,164	27	2.3
Laborers	3,088	277	9.0	2,414	243	10.1	674	34	5.0
Service workers	227	5	2.2	220	5	2.3	7	—	—
Total blue collar	12,579	920	7.3	10,626	859	8.1	1,953	61	3.1
Total	15,042	927	6.2	12,325	864	7.0	2,717	63	2.3

Source: U.S. Equal Employment Opportunity Commission, 1967.

TABLE A-43. *Furniture Industry*

Employment by Race, Sex, and Occupational Group

81 Establishments, Pennsylvania, 1969

Occupational Group	All Employees			Male			Female		
	Total	Negro	Percent Negro	Total	Negro	Percent Negro	Total	Negro	Percent Negro
Officials and managers	1,139	15	1.3	1,102	14	1.3	37	1	2.7
Professionals	127	1	0.8	121	1	0.8	6	—	—
Technicians	244	2	0.8	222	2	0.9	22	—	—
Sales workers	242	1	0.4	205	1	0.5	37	—	—
Office and clerical workers	1,371	44	3.2	426	25	5.9	945	19	2.0
Total white collar	3,123	63	2.0	2,076	43	2.1	1,047	20	1.9
Craftsmen	3,206	272	8.5	2,976	263	8.8	230	9	3.9
Operatives	7,493	926	12.4	6,074	678	11.2	1,419	248	17.5
Laborers	3,224	470	14.6	2,640	456	17.3	584	14	2.4
Service workers	363	5	1.4	332	5	1.5	31	—	—
Total blue collar	14,286	1,673	11.7	12,022	1,402	11.7	2,264	271	12.0
Total	17,409	1,736	10.0	14,098	1,445	10.2	3,311	291	8.8

Source: U.S. Equal Employment Opportunity Commission, 1969.

TABLE A-44. *Furniture Industry*
Employment by Race, Sex, and Occupational Group
78 Establishments, Pennsylvania, 1970

Occupational Group	All Employees			Male			Female		
	Total	Negro	Percent Negro	Total	Negro	Percent Negro	Total	Negro	Percent Negro
Officials and managers	1,186	14	1.2	1,148	13	1.1	38	1	2.6
Professionals	141	2	1.4	134	1	0.7	7	1	14.3
Technicians	265	8	3.0	247	8	3.2	18	—	—
Sales workers	270	—	—	233	—	—	37	—	—
Office and clerical workers	1,065	26	2.4	248	5	2.0	817	21	2.6
Total white collar	2,927	50	1.7	2,010	27	1.3	917	23	2.5
Craftsmen	2,714	79	2.9	2,435	65	2.7	279	14	5.0
Operatives	7,254	609	8.4	5,306	510	9.6	1,948	99	5.1
Laborers	3,366	306	9.1	2,561	277	10.8	805	29	3.6
Service workers	255	19	7.5	236	18	7.6	19	1	5.3
Total blue collar	13,589	1,013	7.5	10,538	870	8.3	3,051	143	4.7
Total	16,516	1,063	6.4	12,548	897	7.1	3,968	166	4.2

Source: U.S. Equal Employment Opportunity Commission, 1970.

TABLE A-45. *Furniture Industry*
Employment by Race, Sex, and Occupational Group
63 Establishments, Illinois, 1966

Occupational Group	All Employees			Male			Female		
	Total	Negro	Percent Negro	Total	Negro	Percent Negro	Total	Negro	Percent Negro
Officials and managers	1,252	12	1.0	1,217	11	0.9	35	1	2.9
Professionals	185	1	0.5	170	1	0.6	15	—	—
Technicians	258	2	0.8	248	2	0.8	10	—	—
Sales workers	446	—	—	408	—	—	38	—	—
Office and clerical workers	2,019	42	2.1	565	21	3.7	1,454	21	1.4
Total white collar	4,160	57	1.4	2,608	35	1.3	1,552	22	1.4
Craftsmen	2,528	281	11.1	2,126	230	10.8	402	51	12.7
Operatives	6,441	1,566	24.3	5,164	1,293	25.0	1,277	273	21.4
Laborers	2,300	612	26.6	1,792	506	28.2	508	106	20.9
Service workers	171	28	16.4	157	25	15.9	14	3	21.4
Total blue collar	11,440	2,487	21.7	9,239	2,054	22.2	2,201	433	19.7
Total	15,600	2,544	16.3	11,847	2,089	17.6	3,753	455	12.1

Source: U.S. Equal Employment Opportunity Commission, 1966.

TABLE A-46. *Furniture Industry*
Employment by Race, Sex, and Occupational Group
67 Establishments, Illinois, 1967

Occupational Group	All Employees			Male			Female		
	Total	Negro	Percent Negro	Total	Negro	Percent Negro	Total	Negro	Percent Negro
Officials and managers	1,238	20	1.6	1,201	19	1.6	37	1	2.7
Professionals	223	2	0.9	206	2	1.0	17	—	—
Technicians	224	2	0.9	207	2	1.0	17	—	—
Sales workers	476	—	—	461	—	—	15	—	—
Office and clerical workers	1,893	47	2.5	494	25	5.1	1,399	22	1.6
Total white collar	4,054	71	1.8	2,569	48	1.9	1,485	23	1.5
Craftsmen	3,066	483	15.8	2,520	413	16.4	546	70	12.8
Operatives	5,925	1,257	21.2	4,309	974	22.6	1,616	283	17.5
Laborers	2,959	825	27.9	2,085	605	29.0	874	220	25.2
Service workers	221	40	18.1	192	36	18.8	29	4	13.8
Total blue collar	12,171	2,605	21.4	9,106	2,028	22.3	3,065	577	18.8
Total	16,225	2,676	16.5	11,675	2,076	17.8	4,550	600	13.2

Source: U.S. Equal Employment Opportunity Commission, 1967.

TABLE A-47. *Furniture Industry*
Employment by Race, Sex, and Occupational Group
71 Establishments, Illinois, 1969

Occupational Group	All Employees			Male			Female		
	Total	Negro	Percent Negro	Total	Negro	Percent Negro	Total	Negro	Percent Negro
Officials and managers	1,230	30	2.4	1,180	29	2.5	50	1	2.0
Professionals	418	2	0.5	402	2	0.5	16	—	—
Technicians	348	10	2.9	318	9	2.8	30	1	3.3
Sales workers	436	—	—	413	—	—	23	—	—
Office and clerical workers	1,837	48	2.6	405	27	6.7	1,432	21	1.5
Total white collar	4,269	90	2.1	2,718	67	2.5	1,551	23	1.5
Craftsmen	1,989	382	19.2	1,541	263	17.1	448	119	26.6
Operatives	3,980	850	21.4	2,911	617	21.2	1,069	233	21.8
Laborers	2,308	625	27.1	1,544	442	28.6	764	183	24.0
Service workers	130	32	24.6	123	31	25.2	7	1	14.3
Total blue collar	8,407	1,889	22.5	6,119	1,353	22.1	2,288	536	23.4
Total	12,676	1,979	15.6	8,837	1,420	16.1	3,839	559	14.6

Source: U.S. Equal Employment Opportunity Commission, 1969.

TABLE A-48. *Furniture Industry*
Employment by Race, Sex, and Occupational Group
65 Establishments, Illinois, 1970

Occupational Group	All Employees			Male			Female		
	Total	Negro	Percent Negro	Total	Negro	Percent Negro	Total	Negro	Percent Negro
Officials and managers	1,393	53	3.8	1,320	44	3.3	73	9	12.3
Professionals	481	3	0.6	458	3	0.7	23	—	—
Technicians	373	5	1.3	331	5	1.5	42	—	—
Sales workers	491	—	—	471	—	—	20	—	—
Office and clerical workers	2,016	41	2.0	427	23	5.4	1,589	18	1.1
Total white collar	4,754	102	2.1	3,007	75	2.5	1,747	27	1.5
Craftsmen	2,269	476	21.0	1,693	313	18.5	576	163	28.3
Operatives	4,581	966	21.1	3,548	737	20.8	1,033	229	22.2
Laborers	2,036	640	31.4	1,492	456	30.6	544	184	33.8
Service workers	161	36	22.4	147	33	22.4	14	3	21.4
Total blue collar	9,047	2,118	23.4	6,880	1,539	22.4	2,167	579	26.7
Total	13,801	2,220	16.1	9,887	1,614	16.3	3,914	606	15.5

Source: U.S. Equal Employment Opportunity Commission, 1970.

TABLE A-49. *Furniture Industry*
Employment by Race, Sex, and Occupational Group
50 Establishments, Virginia, 1966

Occupational Group	All Employees			Male			Female		
	Total	Negro	Percent Negro	Total	Negro	Percent Negro	Total	Negro	Percent Negro
Officials and managers	1,133	3	0.3	1,124	3	0.3	9	—	—
Professionals	103	—	—	97	—	—	6	—	—
Technicians	198	1	0.5	188	1	0.5	10	—	—
Sales workers	142	—	—	134	—	—	8	—	—
Office and clerical workers	1,275	16	1.3	300	11	3.7	975	5	0.5
Total white collar	2,851	20	0.7	1,843	15	0.8	1,008	5	0.5
Craftsmen	4,562	497	10.9	4,362	492	11.3	200	5	2.5
Operatives	6,350	893	14.1	5,550	817	14.7	800	76	9.5
Laborers	5,703	2,211	38.8	4,505	1,640	36.4	1,198	571	47.7
Service workers	315	137	43.5	299	126	42.1	16	11	68.8
Total blue collar	16,930	3,738	22.1	14,716	3,075	20.9	2,214	663	29.9
Total	19,781	3,758	19.0	16,559	3,090	18.7	3,222	668	20.7

Source: U.S. Equal Employment Opportunity Commission, 1966.

TABLE A-50. *Furniture Industry*
Employment by Race, Sex, and Occupational Group
55 Establishments, Virginia, 1967

Occupational Group	All Employees			Male			Female		
	Total	Negro	Percent Negro	Total	Negro	Percent Negro	Total	Negro	Percent Negro
Officials and managers	1,267	6	0.5	1,249	6	0.5	18	—	—
Professionals	113	—	—	103	—	—	10	—	—
Technicians	148	—	—	141	—	—	7	—	—
Sales workers	197	1	0.5	194	1	0.5	3	—	—
Office and clerical workers	1,344	16	1.2	301	9	3.0	1,043	7	0.7
Total white collar	3,069	23	0.7	1,988	16	0.8	1,081	7	0.6
Craftsmen	4,896	598	12.2	4,631	581	12.5	265	17	6.4
Operatives	6,806	1,215	17.9	5,521	1,043	18.9	1,285	172	13.4
Laborers	6,799	2,572	37.8	4,961	1,764	35.6	1,838	808	44.0
Service workers	326	166	50.9	302	149	49.3	24	17	70.8
Total blue collar	18,827	4,551	24.2	15,415	3,537	22.9	3,412	1,014	29.7
Total	21,896	4,574	20.9	17,403	3,553	20.4	4,493	1,021	22.7

Source: U.S. Equal Employment Opportunity Commission, 1967.

TABLE A-51. *Furniture Industry*
Employment by Race, Sex, and Occupational Group
52 Establishments, Virginia, 1969

Occupational Group	All Employees			Male			Female		
	Total	Negro	Percent Negro	Total	Negro	Percent Negro	Total	Negro	Percent Negro
Officials and managers	1,417	10	0.7	1,400	10	0.7	17	—	—
Professionals	96	1	1.0	84	1	1.2	12	—	—
Technicians	123	2	1.6	114	2	1.8	9	—	—
Sales workers	198	—	—	198	—	—	—	—	—
Office and clerical workers	1,184	18	1.5	198	9	4.5	986	9	0.9
Total white collar	3,018	31	1.0	1,994	22	1.1	1,024	9	0.9
Craftsmen	5,007	737	14.7	4,724	662	14.0	283	75	26.5
Operatives	6,865	1,790	26.0	5,142	1,339	26.0	1,723	451	26.2
Laborers	6,053	2,329	38.5	3,913	1,332	34.0	2,140	997	46.6
Service workers	275	100	36.4	253	82	32.4	22	18	81.8
Total blue collar	18,200	4,956	27.2	14,032	3,415	24.3	4,168	1,541	37.0
Total	21,218	4,987	23.5	16,026	3,437	21.4	5,192	1,550	29.9

Source: U.S. Equal Employment Opportunity Commission, 1969.

TABLE A-52. *Furniture Industry*
Employment by Race, Sex, and Occupational Group
55 Establishments, Virginia, 1970

Occupational Group	All Employees			Male			Female		
	Total	Negro	Percent Negro	Total	Negro	Percent Negro	Total	Negro	Percent Negro
Officials and managers	1,184	15	1.3	1,169	15	1.3	15	—	—
Professionals	116	1	0.9	107	1	0.9	9	—	—
Technicians	168	3	1.8	158	2	1.3	10	1	10.0
Sales workers	221	—	—	221	—	—	—	—	—
Office and clerical workers	1,117	20	1.8	183	5	2.7	934	15	1.6
Total white collar	2,806	39	1.4	1,838	23	1.3	968	16	1.7
Craftsmen	4,852	653	13.5	4,512	580	12.9	340	73	21.5
Operatives	6,860	2,085	30.4	4,970	1,490	30.0	1,890	595	31.5
Laborers	5,668	2,272	40.1	3,437	1,288	37.5	2,231	984	44.1
Service workers	269	97	36.1	253	84	33.2	16	13	81.3
Total blue collar	17,649	5,107	28.9	13,172	3,442	26.1	4,477	1,665	37.2
Total	20,455	5,146	25.2	15,010	3,465	23.1	5,445	1,681	30.9

Source: U.S. Equal Employment Opportunity Commission, 1970.

TABLE A-53. *Furniture Industry*
Employment by Race, Sex, and Occupational Group
62 Establishments, Indiana, 1966

Occupational Group	All Employees			Male			Female		
	Total	Negro	Percent Negro	Total	Negro	Percent Negro	Total	Negro	Percent Negro
Officials and managers	1,152	—	—	1,128	—	—	24	—	—
Professionals	132	—	—	130	—	—	2	—	—
Technicians	176	—	—	165	—	—	11	—	—
Sales workers	258	—	—	234	—	—	24	—	—
Office and clerical workers	1,191	3	0.3	335	1	0.3	856	2	0.2
Total white collar	2,909	3	0.1	1,992	1	0.1	917	2	0.2
Craftsmen	3,479	27	0.8	3,034	23	0.8	445	4	0.9
Operatives	8,182	176	2.2	6,410	109	1.7	1,772	67	3.8
Laborers	4,021	45	1.1	2,989	41	1.4	1,032	4	0.4
Service workers	313	10	3.2	274	6	2.2	39	4	10.3
Total blue collar	15,995	258	1.6	12,707	179	1.4	3,288	79	2.4
Total	18,904	261	1.4	14,699	180	1.2	4,205	81	1.9

Source: U.S. Equal Employment Opportunity Commission, 1966.

TABLE A-54. *Furniture Industry*
Employment by Race, Sex, and Occupational Group
73 Establishments, Indiana, 1967

Occupational Group	All Employees			Male			Female		
	Total	Negro	Percent Negro	Total	Negro	Percent Negro	Total	Negro	Percent Negro
Officials and managers	1,260	1	0.1	1,227	1	0.1	33	—	—
Professionals	151	—	—	144	—	—	7	—	—
Technicians	199	2	1.0	193	2	1.0	6	—	—
Sales workers	268	—	—	240	—	—	28	—	—
Office and clerical workers	1,328	2	0.2	347	—	—	981	2	0.2
Total white collar	3,206	5	0.2	2,151	3	0.1	1,055	2	0.2
Craftsmen	2,777	28	1.0	2,468	24	1.0	309	4	1.3
Operatives	9,297	189	2.0	6,797	116	1.7	2,500	73	2.9
Laborers	4,511	110	2.4	2,915	100	3.4	1,596	10	0.6
Service workers	299	18	6.0	256	14	5.5	43	4	9.3
Total blue collar	16,884	345	2.0	12,436	254	2.0	4,448	91	2.0
Total	20,090	350	1.7	14,587	257	1.8	5,503	93	1.7

Source: U.S. Equal Employment Opportunity Commission, 1967.

TABLE A-55. *Furniture Industry*
Employment by Race, Sex, and Occupational Group
77 Establishments, Indiana, 1969

Occupational Group	All Employees			Male			Female		
	Total	Negro	Percent Negro	Total	Negro	Percent Negro	Total	Negro	Percent Negro
Officials and managers	1,647	6	0.4	1,611	6	0.4	36	—	—
Professionals	212	—	—	197	—	—	15	—	—
Technicians	287	1	0.3	272	1	0.4	15	—	—
Sales workers	361	—	—	325	—	—	36	—	—
Office and clerical workers	1,681	14	0.8	424	—	—	1,257	14	1.1
Total white collar	4,188	21	0.5	2,829	7	0.2	1,359	14	1.0
Craftsmen	2,642	46	1.7	2,314	39	1.7	328	7	2.1
Operatives	9,647	273	2.8	6,369	162	2.5	3,278	111	3.4
Laborers	6,018	200	3.3	3,638	134	3.7	2,380	66	2.8
Service workers	325	26	8.0	257	21	8.2	68	5	7.4
Total blue collar	18,632	545	2.9	12,578	356	2.8	6,054	189	3.1
Total	22,820	566	2.5	15,407	363	2.4	7,413	203	2.7

Source: U.S. Equal Employment Opportunity Commission, 1969.

TABLE A-56. *Furniture Industry*
Employment by Race, Sex, and Occupational Group
80 Establishments, Indiana, 1970

Occupational Group	All Employees			Male			Female		
	Total	Negro	Percent Negro	Total	Negro	Percent Negro	Total	Negro	Percent Negro
Officials and managers	1,347	3	0.2	1,315	3	0.2	32	—	—
Professionals	162	—	—	137	—	—	25	—	—
Technicians	241	1	0.4	230	—	—	11	1	**9.1**
Sales workers	221	—	—	200	—	—	21	—	—
Office and clerical workers	1,188	6	0.5	297	1	0.3	891	5	0.6
Total white collar	3,159	10	0.3	2,179	4	0.2	980	6	0.6
Craftsmen	1,869	24	1.3	1,638	21	1.3	231	3	1.3
Operatives	7,185	120	1.7	4,829	78	1.6	2,356	42	1.8
Laborers	4,107	115	2.8	2,535	38	1.5	1,572	77	4.9
Service workers	337	15	4.5	306	10	3.3	31	5	16.1
Total blue collar	13,498	274	2.0	9,308	147	1.6	4,190	127	3.0
Total	16,657	284	1.7	11,487	151	1.3	5,170	133	2.6

Source: U.S. Equal Employment Opportunity Commission, 1970.

TABLE A-57. *Furniture Industry*
Employment by Race, Sex, and Occupational Group
40 Establishments, Tennessee, 1966

Occupational Group	All Employees			Male			Female		
	Total	Negro	Percent Negro	Total	Negro	Percent Negro	Total	Negro	Percent Negro
Officials and managers	601	6	1.0	585	6	1.0	16	—	—
Professionals	115	—	—	109	—	—	6	—	—
Technicians	89	—	—	73	—	—	16	—	—
Sales workers	270	—	—	267	—	—	3	—	—
Office and clerical workers	760	18	2.4	210	11	5.2	550	7	1.3
Total white collar	1,835	24	1.3	1,244	17	1.4	591	7	1.2
Craftsmen	1,539	51	3.3	1,363	40	2.9	176	11	6.3
Operatives	6,276	989	15.8	5,288	651	12.3	988	338	34.2
Laborers	4,214	997	23.7	3,367	753	22.4	847	244	28.8
Service workers	199	69	34.7	167	58	34.7	32	11	34.4
Total blue collar	12,228	2,106	17.2	10,185	1,502	14.7	2,043	604	29.6
Total	14,063	2,130	15.1	11,429	1,519	13.3	2,634	611	23.2

Source: U.S. Equal Employment Opportunity Commission, 1966.

TABLE A-58. *Furniture Industry*
Employment by Race, Sex, and Occupational Group
45 Establishments, Tennessee, 1967

Occupational Group	All Employees			Male			Female		
	Total	Negro	Percent Negro	Total	Negro	Percent Negro	Total	Negro	Percent Negro
Officials and managers	790	7	0.9	774	7	0.9	16	—	—
Professionals	124	1	0.8	114	—	—	10	1	10.0
Technicians	75	1	1.3	63	1	1.6	12	—	—
Sales workers	314	—	—	307	—	—	7	—	—
Office and clerical workers	811	24	3.0	234	19	8.1	577	5	0.9
Total white collar	2,114	33	1.6	1,492	27	1.8	622	6	1.0
Craftsmen	1,624	83	5.1	1,523	73	4.8	101	10	9.9
Operatives	8,061	1,312	16.3	6,128	767	12.5	1,933	545	28.2
Laborers	3,558	725	20.4	2,699	535	19.8	859	190	22.1
Service workers	174	39	22.4	158	35	22.2	16	4	25.0
Total blue collar	13,417	2,159	16.1	10,508	1,410	13.4	2,909	749	25.7
Total	15,531	2,192	14.1	12,000	1,437	12.0	3,531	755	21.4

Source: U.S. Equal Employment Opportunity Commission, 1967.

TABLE A-59. *Furniture Industry*
Employment by Race, Sex, and Occupational Group
44 Establishments, Tennessee, 1969

Occupational Group	All Employees			Male			Female		
	Total	Negro	Percent Negro	Total	Negro	Percent Negro	Total	Negro	Percent Negro
Officials and managers	864	12	1.4	853	12	1.4	11	—	—
Professionals	172	2	1.2	153	1	0.7	19	1	5.3
Technicians	179	3	1.7	171	3	1.8	8	—	—
Sales workers	206	—	—	200	—	—	6	—	—
Office and clerical workers	813	24	3.0	243	13	5.3	570	11	1.9
Total white collar	2,234	41	1.8	1,620	29	1.8	614	12	2.0
Craftsmen	1,222	94	7.7	1,172	77	6.6	50	17	34.0
Operatives	7,613	1,148	15.1	5,826	681	11.7	1,787	467	26.1
Laborers	4,571	860	18.8	2,834	563	19.9	1,737	297	17.1
Service workers	247	64	25.9	227	56	24.7	20	8	40.0
Total blue collar	13,653	2,166	15.9	10,059	1,377	13.7	3,594	789	22.0
Total	15,887	2,207	13.9	11,679	1,406	12.0	4,208	801	19.0

Source: U.S. Equal Employment Opportunity Commission, 1969.

TABLE A-60. *Furniture Industry*
Employment by Race, Sex, and Occupational Group
53 Establishments, Tennessee, 1970

Occupational Group	All Employees			Male			Female		
	Total	Negro	Percent Negro	Total	Negro	Percent Negro	Total	Negro	Percent Negro
Officials and managers	1,099	10	0.9	1,079	10	0.9	20	—	—
Professionals	170	3	1.8	152	2	1.3	18	1	5.6
Technicians	151	3	2.0	143	3	2.1	8	—	—
Sales workers	259	—	—	247	—	—	12	—	—
Office and clerical workers	927	33	3.6	260	19	7.3	667	14	2.1
Total white collar	2,606	49	1.9	1,881	34	1.8	725	15	2.1
Craftsmen	1,892	113	6.0	1,726	91	5.3	166	22	13.3
Operatives	7,546	1,219	16.2	5,559	728	13.1	1,987	491	24.7
Laborers	4,018	900	22.4	2,465	574	23.3	1,553	326	21.0
Service workers	322	76	23.6	292	67	22.9	30	9	30.0
Total blue collar	13,778	2,308	16.8	10,042	1,460	14.5	3,736	848	22.7
Total	16,384	2,357	14.4	11,923	1,494	12.5	4,461	863	19.3

Source: U.S. Equal Employment Opportunity Commission, 1970.

TABLE A-61. *Furniture Industry*
Employment by Race, Sex, and Occupational Group
41 Establishments, Michigan, 1966

Occupational Group	All Employees			Male			Female		
	Total	Negro	Percent Negro	Total	Negro	Percent Negro	Total	Negro	Percent Negro
Officials and managers	1,019	9	0.9	994	9	0.9	25	—	—
Professionals	243	1	0.4	225	1	0.4	18	—	—
Technicians	264	1	0.4	257	1	0.4	7	—	—
Sales workers	346	—	—	325	—	—	21	—	—
Office and clerical workers	1,203	8	0.7	335	5	1.5	868	3	0.3
Total white collar	3,075	19	0.6	2,136	16	0.7	939	3	0.3
Craftsmen	1,965	51	2.6	1,748	35	2.0	217	16	7.4
Operatives	5,744	612	10.7	4,972	535	10.8	772	77	10.0
Laborers	3,217	324	10.1	2,418	247	10.2	799	77	9.6
Service workers	178	3	1.7	170	2	1.2	8	1	12.5
Total blue collar	11,104	990	8.9	9,308	819	8.8	1,796	171	9.5
Total	14,179	1,009	7.1	11,444	835	7.3	2,735	174	6.4

Source: U.S. Equal Employment Opportunity Commission, 1966.

TABLE A-62. *Furniture Industry*
Employment by Race, Sex, and Occupational Group
49 Establishments, Michigan, 1967

Occupational Group	All Employees			Male			Female		
	Total	Negro	Percent Negro	Total	Negro	Percent Negro	Total	Negro	Percent Negro
Officials and managers	1,064	2	0.2	1,043	2	0.2	21	—	—
Professionals	266	1	0.4	255	1	0.4	11	—	—
Technicians	391	2	0.5	380	2	0.5	11	—	—
Sales workers	419	—	—	383	—	—	36	—	—
Office and clerical workers	1,482	13	0.9	367	6	1.6	1,115	7	0.6
Total white collar	3,622	18	0.5	2,428	11	0.5	1,194	7	0.6
Craftsmen	2,739	93	3.4	2,498	82	3.3	241	11	4.6
Operatives	7,037	434	6.2	5,799	324	5.6	1,238	110	8.9
Laborers	2,988	280	9.4	2,035	170	8.4	953	110	11.5
Service workers	331	18	5.4	280	14	5.0	51	4	7.8
Total blue collar	13,095	825	6.3	10,612	590	5.6	2,483	235	9.5
Total	16,717	843	5.0	13,040	601	4.6	3,677	242	6.6

Source: U.S. Equal Employment Opportunity Commission, 1967.

TABLE A-63. *Furniture Industry*
Employment by Race, Sex, and Occupational Group
47 Establishments, Michigan, 1969

Occupational Group	All Employees			Male			Female		
	Total	Negro	Percent Negro	Total	Negro	Percent Negro	Total	Negro	Percent Negro
Officials and managers	1,135	5	0.4	1,100	5	0.5	35	—	—
Professionls	283	—	—	271	—	—	12	—	—
Technicians	395	7	1.8	374	7	1.9	21	—	—
Sales workers	446	1	0.2	391	1	0.3	55	—	—
Office and clerical workers	1,415	15	1.1	391	3	0.8	1,024	12	1.2
Total white collar	3,674	28	0.8	2,527	16	0.6	1,147	12	1.0
Craftsmen	2,041	89	4.4	1,938	82	4.2	103	7	6.8
Operatives	6,039	401	6.6	4,972	306	6.2	1,067	95	8.9
Laborers	3,191	333	10.4	1,969	168	8.5	1,222	165	13.5
Service workers	285	16	5.6	223	12	5.4	62	4	6.5
Total blue collar	11,556	839	7.3	9,102	568	6.2	2,454	271	11.0
Total	15,230	867	5.7	11,629	584	5.0	3,601	283	7.9

Source: U.S. Equal Employment Opportunity Commission, 1969.

TABLE A-64. *Furniture Industry*
Employment by Race, Sex, and Occupational Group
50 Establishments, Michigan, 1970

Occupational Group	All Employees			Male			Female		
	Total	Negro	Percent Negro	Total	Negro	Percent Negro	Total	Negro	Percent Negro
Officials and managers	1,253	6	0.5	1,208	6	0.5	45	—	—
Professionals	350	3	0.9	324	3	0.9	26	—	—
Technicians	432	6	1.4	412	6	1.5	20	—	—
Sales workers	448	2	0.4	388	2	0.5	60	—	—
Office and clerical workers	1,573	28	1.8	433	6	1.4	1,140	22	1.9
Total white collar	4,056	45	1.1	2,765	23	0.8	1,291	22	1.7
Craftsmen	2,090	81	3.9	2,007	75	3.7	83	6	7.2
Operatives	5,924	449	7.6	4,917	346	7.0	1,007	103	10.2
Laborers	3,622	319	8.8	2,190	142	6.5	1,432	177	12.4
Service workers	243	17	7.0	199	16	8.0	44	1	2.3
Total blue collar	11,879	866	7.3	9,313	579	6.2	2,566	287	11.2
Total	15,935	911	5.7	12,078	602	5.0	3,857	309	8.0

Source: U.S. Equal Employment Opportunity Commission, 1970.

TABLE A-65. *Furniture Industry*
Employment by Race, Sex, and Occupational Group
43 Establishments, Ohio, 1966

Occupational Group	All Employees			Male			Female		
	Total	Negro	Percent Negro	Total	Negro	Percent Negro	Total	Negro	Percent Negro
Officials and managers	1,325	2	0.2	1,062	2	0.2	263	—	—
Professionals	198	2	1.0	183	2	1.1	15	—	—
Technicians	335	7	2.1	319	6	1.9	16	1	6.3
Sales workers	294	—	—	276	—	—	18	—	—
Office and clerical workers	1,268	16	1.3	454	4	0.9	814	12	1.5
Total white collar	3,420	27	0.8	2,294	14	0.6	1,126	13	1.2
Craftsmen	1,967	132	6.7	1,796	123	6.8	171	9	5.3
Operatives	3,824	265	6.9	3,223	230	7.1	601	35	5.8
Laborers	2,382	336	14.1	2,018	307	15.2	364	29	8.0
Service workers	164	27	16.5	149	26	17.4	15	1	6.7
Total blue collar	8,337	760	9.1	7,186	686	9.5	1,151	74	6.4
Total	11,757	787	6.7	9,480	700	7.4	2,277	87	3.8

Source: U.S. Equal Employment Opportunity Commission, 1966.

TABLE A-66. *Furniture Industry*
Employment by Race, Sex, and Occupational Group
47 Establishments, Ohio, 1967

Occupational Group	All Employees			Male			Female		
	Total	Negro	Percent Negro	Total	Negro	Percent Negro	Total	Negro	Percent Negro
Officials and managers	808	2	0.2	766	2	0.3	42	—	—
Professionals	184	—	—	175	—	—	9	—	—
Technicians	309	8	2.6	298	7	2.3	11	1	9.1
Sales workers	387	—	—	382	—	—	5	—	—
Office and clerical workers	1,243	57	4.6	399	13	3.3	844	44	5.2
Total white collar	2,931	67	2.3	2,020	22	1.1	911	45	4.9
Craftsmen	2,122	239	11.3	1,920	216	11.3	202	23	11.4
Operatives	4,237	370	8.7	3,469	340	9.8	768	30	3.9
Laborers	1,882	165	8.8	1,505	158	10.5	377	7	1.9
Service workers	185	41	22.2	168	37	22.0	17	4	23.5
Total blue collar	8,426	815	9.7	7,062	751	10.6	1,364	64	4.7
Total	11,357	882	7.8	9,082	773	8.5	2,275	109	4.8

Source: U.S. Equal Employment Opportunity Commission, 1967.

TABLE A-67. *Furniture Industry*
Employment by Race, Sex, and Occupational Group
42 Establishments, Ohio, 1969

Occupational Group	All Employees			Male			Female		
	Total	Negro	Percent Negro	Total	Negro	Percent Negro	Total	Negro	Percent Negro
Officials and managers	795	4	0.5	763	4	0.5	32	—	—
Professionals	142	1	0.7	134	1	0.7	8	—	—
Technicians	293	2	0.7	288	2	0.7	5	—	—
Sales workers	351	—	—	341	—	—	10	—	—
Office and clerical workers	1,041	26	2.5	272	6	2.2	769	20	2.6
Total white collar	2,622	33	1.3	1,798	13	0.7	824	20	2.4
Craftsmen	1,419	107	7.5	1,298	99	7.6	121	8	6.6
Operatives	3,778	258	6.8	3,022	203	6.7	756	55	7.3
Laborers	1,918	199	10.4	1,489	165	11.1	429	34	7.9
Service workers	168	33	19.6	148	27	18.2	20	6	30.0
Total blue collar	7,283	597	8.2	5,957	494	8.3	1,326	103	7.8
Total	9,905	630	6.4	7,755	507	6.5	2,150	123	5.7

Source: U.S. Equal Employment Opportunity Commission, 1969.

TABLE A-68. *Furniture Industry*
Employment by Race, Sex, and Occupational Group
45 Establishments, Ohio, 1970

Occupational Group	All Employees			Male			Female		
	Total	Negro	Percent Negro	Total	Negro	Percent Negro	Total	Negro	Percent Negro
Officials and managers	811	9	1.1	782	9	1.2	29	—	—
Professionals	183	1	0.5	171	1	0.6	12	—	—
Technicians	308	5	1.6	293	5	1.7	15	—	—
Sales workers	345	—	—	344	—	—	1	—	—
Office and clerical workers	1,105	30	2.7	242	3	1.2	863	27	3.1
Total white collar	2,752	45	1.6	1,832	18	1.0	920	27	2.9
Craftsmen	1,482	130	8.8	1,358	120	8.8	124	10	8.1
Operatives	4,521	302	6.7	3,583	236	6.6	938	66	7.0
Laborers	1,535	171	11.1	929	135	14.5	606	36	5.9
Service workers	138	37	26.8	116	29	25.0	22	8	36.4
Total blue collar	7,676	640	8.3	5,986	520	8.7	1,690	120	7.1
Total	10,428	685	6.6	7,818	538	6.9	2,610	147	5.6

Source: U.S. Equal Employment Opportunity Commission, 1970.

Index

AFL, 33-34
Aberdeen, 11
Amalgamated Wood Workers International Union of America (AWW), 33
Armstrong Cork, 10

Bassett Furniture Industries, 9
Brody, 11
Burlington Industries, 10

CIO, 34
Cabinetmaking in the United States, 36-38
Census data
comparison with EEOC data, 63-64
Civil Rights Act of 1964, 35, 62-63, 123, 128, 133-134
Civil War
effect on the furniture industry, 41

Davis, Kenneth R., 22
Dinsmore, James, 38
Dolly Madison, 10
Drexel enterprises, 11
Duncan Phyfe, 37

Eisenhower, Dwight D., 61
Elfe, Thomas, Jr., 39
Elfe, Thomas, Sr., 39
Equal Employment Opportunity Commission, 62, 129-130, 133
comparison of EEOC and census data, 63-64
European immigrants
employment in the furniture industry, 36, 131
Executive Order 8802, 61
Executive Order 10925, 62
Executive Order 11246, 62

Fisher, John, 39
Furniture industry
and government pressure, 62, 129-130, 133-134
customer orientation, 17
earnings and hours, 28-29
ease of entry, 9, 11

emergence of the furniture factory, 40-42
employment trends, 67-68
employment trends, by category
craftsmen, 75-76
laborers, 78
office and clerical workers, 74-75
officials and managers, 69-70
operatives, 76-77
professionals and technicians, 72-73
sales workers, 73-74
service workers, 78-79
employment trends, by region,
California, 120
Illinois, 110-111
Indiana, 111-114
Michigan, 114-116
Middle Atlantic States, 86-93
Midwest, 107-118
New England, 83-84
New York, 91-93
North Carolina, 100-102, 106
Ohio, 116-118
Pennsylvania, 93
South, 83, 95-107, 124, 129
Tennessee, 104-106
Virginia, 102-104
West, 118-120
entry of conglomerates, 9-11, 82
effect on employment practices, 135
general characteristics, 2, 4-5, 7, 9
history and development, 36-60
industrial growth, 12, 15, 17
industrial location, 17-21
integration of facilities, 127-128
intraplant movement of workers, 79
merger movement, 9-11
movement to the South, 18, 42-48, 95
occupational distribution, 22-26
production processes, 3-4
prospects for the future, 136
seniority systems, 134
size and number of establishments, 7-9, 63

205